HandyMa'am®:

Home Improvement, Decorating, & Maintenance Tips & Projects for You and Your Family

HandyMa'am®:

Home Improvement, Decorating, & Maintenance Tips & Projects for You and Your Family

by Beverly DeJulio

Companion to the Public Television Series

Real Estate Education Company®
A Kaplan Professional Company

This publication is designed to provide accurate and authoritative information in regard to the subject matter covered. It is sold with the understanding that the publisher is not engaged in rendering legal, accounting, or other professional service. If legal advice or other expert assistance is required, the services of a competent professional person should be sought.

IMPORTANT INFORMATION: The publisher and author have made every effort to ensure that the information, diagrams, and photographs contained in this book are accurate. In doing any home project, the reader should plan thoroughly and carefully assess his or her own skill level, tools, and local conditions and materials. Due to the variation in skills, tools, conditions, and materials, the publisher and author assume no responsibility for any injuries or losses resulting from the reader's use of the information contained in this publication. The reader should always follow appropriate safety precautions, local codes and laws, and manufacturer's instructions and recommendations for use of equipment and other materials. In the event of questions, the reader should not hesitate to contact local and other home improvement sources, some of which have been referenced in this publication.

Editorial Director: Cynthia A. Zigmund
Acquisitions Editor: Jean Iversen
Managing Editor: Jack Kiburz
Interior Design: Preface, Inc.
Cover Design: Scott Rattray, Rattray Design
Cover Photo: © Paul Natkin/Window to the World Communications, Inc.
Interior Photos: © Window to the World Communications, Inc./Ms. Fix-It, Inc.
Illustrations: Precision Graphics

© 1999 by Window to the World Communications, Inc. and Ms. Fix-It, Inc.

Published by Real Estate Education Company®,
a Kaplan Professional Company

Printed in the United States of America

99 00 01 10 9 8 7 6 5 4 3 2 1

Library of Congress Cataloging-in-Publication Data

DeJulio, Beverly.
    HandyMa'am : home improvement, decorating, & maintenance tips & projects for you and your family / Beverly DeJulio.
        p. cm.
    Includes index.
    ISBN 0-7931-3341-6 (case)
    1. Dwellings–Maintenance and repair–Amateurs' manuals.
    2. Interior decoration–Amateurs' manuals. I. Title. II. Title: HandyMa'am III. Title: Home improvement, decorating, & maintenance tips & projects for you and your family
    TH4817.3 .D42 1999
    643'.7–dc21   98-52978
                                            CIP

Real Estate Education Company books are available at special quantity discounts to use as premiums and sales promotions, or for use in corporate training programs. For more information, please call the Special Sales Manager at 800-621-9621, ext. 4514, or write to Dearborn Financial Publishing, Inc., 155 North Wacker Drive, Chicago, IL 60606-1719

Contents

Acknowledgments

There are so many people that need to be thanked for their help and support: *HandyMa'am®: Home Improvement, Decorating, & Maintenance Tips & Projects for You and Your Family* is very much the happy by-product of many years of personal and professional experience. From the first time that I threaded a needle to my first walk into a hardware store, countless people from all walks of life have enabled me to acquire the skills and self-belief necessary to "do it" myself. Actually, I'm even indebted to those who did NOT believe in me or any woman's ability to tackle a home improvement or maintenance project, for their doubt helped fire my determination to make it happen (even so, we'll just leave them nameless!).

First, I want to acknowledge Mary Beth Hughes, Fred Schneider, Jay Smith, and Tim Ward of WTTW's Chicago Production Center, as well as their very talented staff and crew, for believing in the HandyMa'am® project and making it a reality. From designing the set, to the day-to-day taping, to the final edits and Web site—it's been a real team effort, each one giving 110 percent and putting in long days. And speaking of team effort and long days, on the New Ventures side of WTTW, a big bravo to Katherine Lauderdale, Deana Kobrynski, Christine Callozzo, Marc Glick, and Ron Nigro for going beyond the call of duty in order to make this companion book a reality. I could not have done it without you!

And where would we be without the early belief and financial support of our underwriters—Ace Hardware and Lennox Heating and Cooling? We are so grateful for their generosity and market vision. Thanks for believing in our dream of bringing home improvement "know how," "how to," and "can do" to the PBS market.

And Marci Rubin, dear friend and loyal business partner, thanks for working alongside me and making sure that what needed to happen, happened. I'm so glad that you called WBBM radio all those years ago, saying there must be something we could do together. How right you were!

To WBBM-AM radio—Bob and Betty Sanders, who are responsible for my first experience with the media. What fabulous mentors!

And to Chris and Angel—beyond daughters, business associates extraordinaire—your dedication and countless hours of work, doing "whatever it takes" to get the job done!

And to agent Caroline Carney of Book Deals, Inc. and freelance writer Marc Malkin, a thank you for helping me pull this book together so quickly. It's such a pleasure to see all these projects and wonderful memories captured in print for the first time!

To entertainment lawyer, Linda Mensch—you are always right-on with your guidance.

And to my can-do editor Jean Iversen and all of her dedicated colleagues at Dearborn, including: Editorial Director Cynthia Zigmund, Editorial Assistant Sandy Holzbach; Managing Editor Jack Kiburz; Art Director Lucy Jenkins, and sales and marketing masterminds Paul Mallon and Bobbye Middendorf. Thank you for having the fearless determination and guts to get a high-quality, high-value book onto the market and into so many hands in so little time. You're a powerful team!

And to my Tennessee Family, Cinetel Productions, Cinetel Studios, and HGTV for taking a chance almost ten years ago with a lady who could swing a hammer, but didn't know the first thing about television and which camera to look at! Besides working together and the continuing learning experience, we've been through so much—weddings, births, the loss of loved ones, and everything in between.

To all the viewers who've watched me faithfully through the years. You are the reason we do what we do!

And now, to those of you who have been in my heart for so long, including: The Bridge Group—we were a support group before support groups were popular; brothers (and their families) Chuck, Bob (I know you are with us in spirit), and Steve, you are the best; Mom and Dad who've been the best role models and parents in every way—Mom's simple motto to us: "Can't can't do anything, just try!" (How true is that?!); Michael, Kris (Mark), and Karen who are my step-children and dear friends; Vince, Chris (Michael), Anthony (Stevie), and Angel who are truly blessings from God—your smiling faces, warm hugs, and I love you's make life complete. (Somehow one of you would always make me smile even in the toughest of times.) And to Bill, who is my husband, best friend, and confidant—you help make life's journey much easier and more enjoyable; and to our newest additions, our HandyGrandchildren, Taylor, Kate, Anthony, and Anna who bring so much fun to all our lives. I am so fortunate to have all of you in my life!

Beverly DeJulio

WTTW Acknowledgments

We are incredibly proud of our association with Beverly DeJulio, Christine DeJulio, Executive Producer Marci Rubin, and the rest of the HandyMa'am® family. We hope that the **HandyMa'am®** series and book will empower "handy-challenged" people everywhere to become confident do-it-yourselfers.

Special thanks are extended to the following persons from WTTW who worked on this book: Researcher and Editorial Assistant Deana Kobrynski, Executive Producer Fred Schneider, Producer Jay Smith, Christine Callozzo, Marc Glick, Nettie Riley, and Ron Nigro. We are also extremely grateful to our agent extraordinaire, Caroline Carney; writer and remarkable spirit Marc Malkin; and Cynthia Zigmund, Jean Iversen, and the rest of the patient, talented staff at Dearborn Financial Publishing.

Last, but not least, we thank the Program Underwriters, ACE HARDWARE and LENNOX HEATING AND COOLING, for their generous support, as well as the following people who produced the **HandyMa'am®** television series on which this book is based:

WTTW Management

Daniel Schmidt
President and CEO

Mary Beth Hughes
Sr. VP, The Chicago Production Center

Production Staff

Beverly DeJulio
Host/Exec. Producer

Marci Rubin
Exec. Producer

Frederick Schneider
Exec. Producer

Jay T. Smith
Producer

Tim Ward
Director

Christine DeJulio
Associate Producer

Cynthia Malek
Associate Director

Michelle McKenzie-Voigt
Associate Director

Barbara Scott
Prop Master

Michael Loewenstein
Scenic Design

Fred Burton
Director, Art & Design Services

Steve Larson
Art Director

Gina Morri
Graphic Design

Nettie Riley
Historical Research

Bill McElwee
Master Carpenter

Brian McKee
Carpenter

Al Ortiz
Carpenter

David Tannenbaum
Carpenter

Katie Corcoran
Production Assistant

Angel DeJulio
Production Assistant

Katherine Malone
Production Assistant

Jerry Glover
Legal

Marcia Forbes
Make-up

Shaunese Teamer
Publicist

Marie Considine
Project Manager

Karen Larson
Production Accountant

CAMP Music Co., Inc.
Original Music

**Studio/Post
Production Staff**

Ron Yergovich
Director, Production Operations

Tim Snell
Production Manager

Richard J. Well
Technical Director

Derrick Young
Technical Director

Roy D. Alan
Camera

Al Hilliard
Camera

Cal Langenberg
Camera

Raymond O. Meinke
Camera

Dave Moyer
Camera

Mike Prendergast
Camera

Carlos Tronshaw
Camera

Emmett E. Wilson
Camera

Bob Brunner
Video

Steve Miller
Video

Barbara Allen
Video Tape

Mark Anderson
Video Tape

Rich Davies
Video Tape

Donna Finlon
Video Tape

John Kennamer
Audio

Jim Lindberg
Audio

Jim Mancini
Audio

Marvin J. Pienta
Floor Director

Kim R. Breitenbach
Floor Assistant

Robert Henning
Floor Assistant

Maurice Smith
Floor Assistant

Derrick Thomas
Floor Assistant

Robert Wratschko
Floor Assistant

Jim Gedwellas
Lighting Director

William Alvelo
Lighting Assistant

Rick Moyer
Lighting Assistant

Danny Rozkuszka
Lighting Assistant

Noel Torres
Lighting Assistant

Don DeMartini
Editor

Paul Thornton
Editor

Jerry Binder
Post Production Audio

Robert Dove
Post Production Audio

Barbara Shintani
Electronic Titles

On behalf of WTTW,

Katherine Lauderdale

Katherine Lauderdale
*Sr. Vice President
New Ventures*

Do It Yourself!

It was a clear fall day in 1975, and I was busy doing endless loads of laundry for myself and my four kids (ages nine, seven, four, and two). All of a sudden, I noticed that gallons of sudsy water were about to spill over the top of the sump pump onto the basement floor. We were headed for a major flood! I didn't know what was wrong. I ran and shut off the washing machine. What could possibly be wrong? Well, my sump pump was dead!

Most homes in my neighborhood have a sump pit and pump in the basement or crawl space to prevent flooding. Excess ground water accumulates in the pit and, when the water reaches a certain level, the sump pump automatically starts pumping the water into the yard or the storm sewers, depending on local codes. In my house, water from the washing machine drained into the utility sink and then into the sump pit where it was supposed to be pumped up the sewer pipes and out of the house.

Well, on that autumn morning, after I realized my sump pump was dead, I sat on the basement stairs and cried. I was newly divorced and didn't know the first thing about fixing a sump pump. I never thought I'd need to know.

I grew up in a small town about 90 miles from Chicago. Back then, roles for men and women were clearly defined. Women were expected to get married, have children, and be stay-at-home moms. Men were the ones who were supposed to go out and make the money and, when they were home, they were supposed to fix and build things around the house. The only "machinery" women were expected to use were kitchen appliances—an iron, a vacuum, a sewing machine, or a hair dryer.

Well, I did *some* of what was expected of me. In 1963, I married, and 12 years later, I was a divorced single mom raising four kids. My world, needless to say, wasn't turning out the way I'd envisioned. However, I wasn't about to let that get in my way. Sure, single motherhood was something I had to get used to and divorce is never an easy thing. But I looked at the changes in my life as a sign that it was time to move on to a new phase in my family's life. I knew, as did my family and friends, that there was no way I'd let change—no matter how big or small— overcome me and leave me paralyzed.

So as I sat on those basement steps, crying my eyes out over a sump pump, I suddenly realized there was no shoulder to cry on. The only person who was going to fix that pump was me. I reminded myself of something I learned when I was a child: God doesn't give us more than we can handle. In other words, I was capable of taking care of this situation.

I started asking my neighbors for advice. Should I repair the pump or replace the whole thing altogether? Most agreed that the pump needed to be replaced.

A Do-It-Yourselfer Is Born

"Great," I thought. "I don't have the money either to buy a new pump or to hire someone to install it." That's when I decided to learn how to do it myself.

I went out and bought a new pump, grilling the salespeople about everything. I wanted to make sure I was getting my money's worth. But when I got home with the new pump, I realized I didn't know how to remove the old one. So, I improvised. I followed the new pump's installation directions backwards. I thought I was in over my head. But through the years I've learned that manufacturers never include instructions on how to remove old appliances. I still rely on following directions backwards.

As I began to install the pump, I realized that new pumps were as unlikely to perfectly connect to the old pipes as the last strip of wallpaper is to match at the final corner. My existing pipe was too short. I went back to the hardware store and sat there as a teenage salesperson explained the difference between male and female pipes. I don't know which one of us was more embarrassed. But I hung in there and returned home with the right connector pipe.

I cannot begin to describe the sense of accomplishment I felt as I made the last connection. I gathered my four kids around the pump and plugged it in. The pump went on. But then we all took an unexpected shower as water blasted through the new pipe.

"Mommy," Anthony, my four-year-old, said to me, "I don't think you fixed it."

Let's just say that from that day on I will never forget that you have to join plumbing pipes with pipe sealant. My children's lesson? They kept at a safe distance whenever I tested a new plumbing job.

I applied the pipe sealant at every connection and once again poured water into the pit. Even though I assured my children that the water would disappear, they insisted on wearing raincoats as I poured the water. (I was kidding about the raincoats, but they did stand way back, just in case!) And much to their surprise—and even mine, I must admit—when the pump kicked in, the water was whisked away.

From that moment on, maintaining my home was no longer as frightening as it had been. When Anthony cried out in amazement, "Mommy, you fixed the pump!" I realized there was nothing at all magical about this repair.

I proved to my kids and myself that I was capable of more than I thought. We were going to make it, and the sump pump was all the proof we needed.

Date _____

Room _____

Project name _____

Project goal _____

Project priority   ☐ Urgent   ☐ Important   ☐ Can wait

Tools needed _____ ☐ on hand   ☐ to buy

_____ ☐ on hand   ☐ to buy

_____ ☐ on hand   ☐ to buy

_____ ☐ on hand   ☐ to buy

_____ ☐ on hand   ☐ to buy

Supplies needed _____ ☐ on hand   ☐ to buy

_____ ☐ on hand   ☐ to buy

_____ ☐ on hand   ☐ to buy

_____ ☐ on hand   ☐ to buy

_____ ☐ on hand   ☐ to buy

**HandyFamily
activity ideas** _____

_____

**Project budget
(include 10%
contingency)** _____

Schedule   start date _____   phase 2 _____

phase 1 _____   completion _____

Other _____

**Notes for future
reference** _____

_____

_____

Plan to Work, Work to Plan

With every new project I'd tackle, it just made the next one easier. Sure, there were frustrating afternoons reading directions that were indecipherable or ones that assumed I knew more than I actually did. But I persevered, and I'm glad I did.

One very valuable lesson I learned through hard experience is that it's so important to read a project's instructions completely and to draw up a plan of action before plunging in. If you've ever cooked a meal or put together a neighborhood block party, you know most things require planning and organization. Household projects are no exception. Eighty percent of any good homemaking project will be spent preparing for the 20 percent that shows. Whether you are painting, tiling, wallpapering, or hanging window treatments, the job won't hold up and look professional without proper preparation.

My tried-and-true approach to organizing homemaking projects is based on this philosophy of St. Francis of Assisi: "Start by doing what's necessary, then what's possible, and suddenly you are doing the impossible." With that in mind, I keep a constantly updated set of three lists. The first list is top-priority tasks. The second list contains things I want to do in the near future—usually decorative or moderately priced improvement projects. The third is my wish list—generally expensive or time-consuming renovation projects or things that will require a lot of concentrated effort and attention. Then, depending on how much time I have and the priority of the items on the list, I select a job and I get to it. Before you plunge into your project, review the checklist on the opposite page. I've found it handy for getting projects started out on the right foot.

I've found that keeping good notes on each of my projects shortens the learning curve for the next time I tackle it, plus it makes the ongoing repair and maintenance a snap.

What's in Store

In the following projects, you'll learn everything there is to know about not only repair, but also about improving and creating beautiful new things for your home. You'll learn what tools work best and what supplies you'll need. And as you do before cooking that meal or organizing a neighborhood celebration, I'll help you assemble everything you need before you begin. (I know you want to make as few runs to the store as possible.)

My directions are easy to use even for you freshmen repair folks. If my instructions conflict with the manufacturer's directions, follow theirs. And make sure to heed their safety precautions. This is such an important point that I've even added some tried-and-true **Play It Safe!** tips to the end of each chapter.

Fun for the Whole Family

Even if my kids did get soaked during my sump pump fiasco, they still love being involved. That's why, throughout the book, you'll find **HandyFamily** projects for children of all ages. While you're working away, your kids can be working on their own projects—ones that are similar to the ones you're working on so they can share your sense of pride and accomplishment.

HandyFriends

Through the years, I've gotten some of my best tips and techniques from friends, relatives, and industry experts. As we go through the book, I'll introduce you to some of my **HandyFriends,** and they'll give you extra pointers on how to save money and time, as well as getting professional-looking results with your homemaking projects.

Simple Solutions

In this chapter, we've talked about how doing it myself really gave a boost to my self-esteem. Well, there have been some other benefits— one hinted at above: Many of these projects have given me the opportunity to spend quality time with my kids and enjoy their company. Also, by doing it ourselves, we've been able to turn our house into a home on a reasonable budget, *and* we've been able to save money on potentially costly repairs and maintenance challenges. Some of my best money- and time-saving ideas you'll see featured on my shows and in this book under the heading **Simple Solutions.** Many of these quick tips also show you easy ways to avoid the pitfalls of do-it-yourself projects—such as knowing what to bring to the hardware store when you're fixing a lamp or how to remove extra grout from your newly tiled bathroom.

Go to It!

Whatever this book accomplishes, I hope it inspires you to do it yourself! Sure, we all have our own personal limits (whether they are money, ability, or time) but, if you're like me, you'll find that you're capable of far more than you ever dreamed. Just remember to be patient with yourself, take your time, and tackle a project only when you're ready.

If you've used an electric handheld mixer, you can use a power drill. If you've ever spread glue on a model airplane, you can caulk around your bathtub. Just keep telling yourself, "I can do it!" Hey, if I could install a sump pump, so can you!

Handy Tools and Adhesives

2

Look up! How many tools do you think it takes to keep that roof over your head from crashing down on you? Actually, it's not as many as you might think. In fact, if you have some basic tools like a hammer, some nails, a screwdriver, and some screws, chances are you're well on your way to having an efficient tool kit. It doesn't take an expensive collection of fancy gizmos and gadgets to maintain a home. In this chapter, I'm going to introduce you to the basic tools and supplies for handling most maintenance chores, minor to moderate repairs, and some really fun and exciting do-it-yourself projects. As your skills develop, I'm sure you'll start looking at some more sophisticated tools. When that time comes, you'll need to choose between renting or buying them. Your decisions will be based on your budget and how many times you think you'll actually be using the specific tool.

Get Organized!

Many people keep their tools together with their kitchen utensils in that black hole most of us call "the junk drawer." The first step to home maintenance and improvement is finding a designated place for your tools. Get out of the habit of storing them with your spatulas, grocery coupons, and other clutter. Sure, you can keep your tools in a kitchen drawer, but make sure this drawer is only for your tools. And, after finishing a project, clean your tools and put them back where they belong. Keeping them clean and organized saves you time, money, and frustration.

Your Toolbox

You can store your tools in anything that works for you. But think about how you work before you make an investment. I travel with my tools, so finding a lightweight case was very important to me. I use a rugged plastic toolbox that's strong enough to protect my tools but not so heavy that it'll cause back strain. It sort of looks like an ice chest, so airport security is always asking me, "Hey, what's in the cooler?"

If you're constantly running back and forth looking for the right-size screwdriver or drill bit, you may want to get a sturdy canvas tote bag. Load up the bag with everything you need before you start a project so you can avoid all those trips to wherever you decided to store your tools.

If you do most of your projects in a separate work-room (like an area in the basement or garage), you may want not only a toolbox, but also some sort of organization system. You can use

Simple Solution

Anytime you're working with small parts—like nuts, bolts, washers, and screws—keep them on a piece of masking tape. This will prevent them from getting "lost" while you're working.

Simple Solution

Keep all your owner's manuals for appliances and tools in one place for easy access. A ring binder or tote box works great!

HANDY FAMILY ACTIVITY

I've found that girls and boys alike love to play with tools. As you put together your own toolbox, why not create one for your kids to use? They could use a small tackle box and a carpenter's apron to hold their tools (and art supplies, for that matter). Most hand tools are safe for children ten years and older to use: Of course, you'll first need to spend some time showing them the proper purpose and handling of each tool. (Using a tape measure helps with math and fractions!) If they're very young, the plastic toy versions of your tools will give them hours of fun and, who knows, they may grow up to become the next Norm Abrams or HandyMa'am®!

pegboard for hanging tools, cabinets for storage, and a workbench. Believe me, the more organized you are, the happier you'll be.

You may want to make a trip to the hardware store while trying to decide what kind of toolbox you want. Look at the different kinds that are out there. They range from simple toolboxes that look like cosmetic cases and lunch boxes to elaborate metal tool cabinets on wheels and roll-up storage devices with compartments that adjust in size. Some boxes are designed to hold specific power tools and their related accessories, like drill cases with different compartments for various bits and power cords or batteries. Others come embossed with commonly needed information such as nail and screw sizes, measurement conversions, straightedges, and rulers. Portable toolboxes generally have an assortment of drawers, compartments, and pockets so you can carry a wide variety of tools, fasteners, and adhesives. The important thing is to find a carrier that'll keep you organized. Nothing's worse than fishing to the bottom of a tote bag filled with hardware to find one little nail.

SCREWDRIVERS Screwdrivers are probably the most often used and *mis*used tools of all. You've probably never given a lot of thought about how to use a screwdriver because it seems so obvious. But actually the right technique will maximize your effort and minimize any hassle. First off, when driving a screw into a vertical surface, position your body so that the screwdriver is being used between your waist and shoulders. This will give your drive maximum force. Also, make sure to keep the blade of the driver in a straight line with the body of the screw. This will help to ensure that you don't strip the screw head.

There are many types of screwdrivers. The two most common are the slotted (also known as flat head or standard screwdrivers) and the Phillips, which has a "cross" tip. You can buy screwdriver sets that have a selection of both Phillips and standard in different sizes. The sizes refer to the size of the tip and the length of the blade. You'll want to have several sizes of each so you'll have the correct size when you need it. If you already own some screwdrivers, check their handles to see if the size is specified; that way you'll know what sizes you have on hand and which you need to buy to round out your basic set of tools.

> ## Simple Solution
>
> **When shopping for a screwdriver—or any tool, for that matter—be sure to hold it in your hand and see how it fits. We try on clothes to see how they fit, why not tools? How well a tool works depends more on how securely it can be gripped than on its price.**

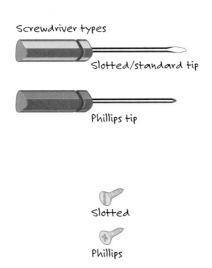

Screwdriver types

Slotted/standard tip

Phillips tip

Slotted

Phillips

For standard, I suggest you get a 3 in. cabinet, 4 in. mechanic, and 6 in. mechanic. For Phillips: a size 2 (which fits screw sizes 5 to 10) and size 1 (for screw sizes 2 to 5). Even though I don't use a size 3 or a size 0 very often, you may want to pick them up anyway, because when I do need them they are the only ones that will work.

AWL   It looks like an ice pick and can be used for making small starter holes for nails, screws, and drill bits. You can use it instead of a pencil to mark where you need to drill or saw. Awls are also used to punch holes in vinyl, leather, and other heavy materials.

Scratch awl

HAMMER   For basic projects, a hammer between 12 oz. and 16 oz. should be just fine. When using a hammer, grasp it with one hand toward the end of the handle—not up by the head—with your fingers and thumb wrapped around the handle. This will give you a more powerful swing. (For the most power, swing from the elbow.) To start, tap the nail lightly just to break the surface. Then use more force with each successive swing. Remember throughout the process to bring the flat head of the hammer into complete contact with the flat head of the nail in order to avoid bending the nail or driving it in at an angle.

Curved-claw hammer

WRENCHES   You should be equipped with two sizes of adjustable wrenches—small and medium—so you don't have to have a different-size wrench for every size nut and bolt.

Adjustable wrench

Metal punching projects are a great way to introduce kids to different tools and to create arts and crafts style accents for your home. Using a punch, nail, or another pointy object and a hammer, your kids can "punch" designs into a piece of tin, copper, or brass. Suggested designs and complete metal punching kits are available at craft stores. Adult supervision is recommended for this project, as are heavy-duty leather work gloves for protection from the metal's sharp corners and edges.

PLIERS   Slip-joint pliers, the most common type, are used for small jobs. Tongue-and-groove pliers adjust to different sizes. Needle-nose pliers are used on very small or delicate items (to hold tiny nails and avoid hitting your fingers), for hard-to-reach places, and to cut and bend wire. I suggest that you invest in one of each type.

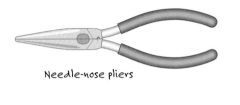

Needle-nose pliers   Slip-joint pliers

Tongue & groove pliers

Simple Solution

Save an old leather belt, glove, rubber inner tube, or rubber glove for lining the jaws of pliers when you need to protect the finish of a surface from the pliers' teeth.

LEVEL   Forget about "eyeballing" a project. Use a level! The only way to ensure that counters, shelves, and pictures are truly horizontal (level) or that cabinets and wallpaper are actually vertical (plumb), is to check the positioning first with a level. The most common levels cost only about $5 and are made of plastic. You simply rest the level on the surface and adjust the surface until the air bubble floating in the level's clear vial is centered between the hatch marks on the level. Using a level is one of the easiest and cheapest ways to get professional-looking results with your projects. Make sure you always have one handy.

Torpedo level

SAFETY GLASSES   And speaking of "eyeballing," protecting your eyesight is job number one. Whenever you use any striking, cutting, or power tools, first don your safety glasses. *No tool box is complete without safety glasses!*

UTILITY KNIFE   You'll need to have a utility knife on hand for cutting, trimming, and scoring. For some jobs, such as cutting carpet or linoleum, you will need to purchase a knife that is designed to cut that specific type of material. Also, I suggest looking into a model that has safety features such as a locking blade function.

Utility knife

RETRACTABLE METAL TAPE MEASURE   HandyMa'am® never leaves home without her tape measure, and you shouldn't either. You never know when you'll need one. Certainly, before investing in a new household item, it often pays to measure first before hauling it home and finding out that it's just not a fit. I do recommend that you invest in a 12-ft. metal tape measure with a locking function to help you get more accurate measurements.

Tape measure

HANDSAW   Some hardware stores and home centers will cut wood for you for a small fee. But if you're going to be cutting a lot of wood at various times, go ahead and invest in a general-purpose saw that can be used for crosscuts (cuts that go across the grain of the wood) and ripcuts (cuts in the same direction of the grain). In any case, the teeth of most handsaws are angled forward away from the handle so they cut on the down stroke. The important rule of thumb for sawing: Cut as you push, not as you pull.

Simple Solution

When measuring, live by the old saying, "Measure twice, cut once!"

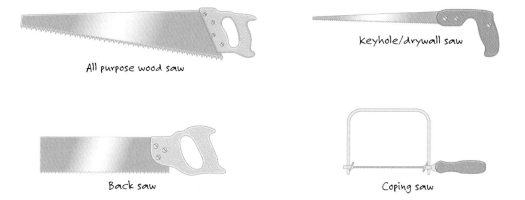

All purpose wood saw

Keyhole/drywall saw

Back saw

Coping saw

Other kinds of basic saws include hacksaws, backsaws (which can be used with a miter box), coping saws, and drywall saws. Each of these saws is either designed to make a specific sort of cut or intended for use on a certain type of building material. The projects in this book will always let you know if a special kind of saw is needed.

UTILITY LIGHT Unfortunately, many household maintenance and repair chores are in out-of-the-way places where it's hard to get to and even harder to see. For these situations, a hands-free utility light is absolutely essential. It's not necessary to spend a lot of money on something fancy: A basic bulb in a protective hook or clamp and a long cord should suffice. Also, you'll want to keep yourself equipped with a working flashlight.

BASIC ANCHORS Anchors are critical when you're hanging any object of significant weight, such as shelves or window treatments. There are many different types, and you'll find it wise to maintain a few of the following in your toolbox.

Plastic Anchors. These will suffice for most of your lightweight jobs, such as hanging pictures or curtain rods. To install these anchors, you'll need to first drill a pilot hole.

Molly Bolt. This anchor-screw combination has to match the thickness of your walls. It's a good bet for medium to heavy jobs, such as installing drapery rods and heavy mirrors. First drill a pilot hole.

Toggle Bolt. For heavy jobs, such as hanging plants, shelving units, or a bicycle from a basement ceiling, professionals swear by toggle bolts. Spring-loaded toggles are a little more difficult to use because the object being hung from the toggle must be attached to it before it is installed into the wall. Plastic toggles prevent this problem. First drill a pilot hole.

> ## Simple Solution
>
> **When working with a new tool, practice using it on a piece of scrap material.**

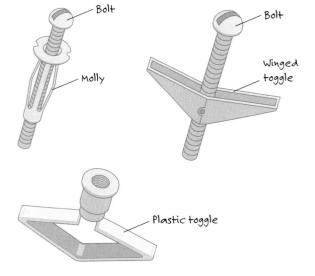

Bolt — Molly

Bolt — Winged toggle

Plastic toggle

POWER TOOLS   No doubt about it: Electric mixers work faster than hand mixers, and electric knives will slice a turkey with a lot less effort on your part than if you use a conventional carving knife. Power tools work the same way. As your skills and confidence grow, you may want to consider purchasing one or more of the following:

- Cordless power screwdriver
- Cordless power drill
- Circular saw
- Jigsaw or saber saw

Simple Solution

Make a stand for your drill bits to keep them from getting dull or damaged. Simply use each drill bit to drill a hole in a scrap piece of two-by-four and mark each hole with the size bit used, so you know which bit goes in each hole.

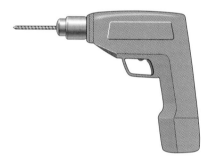

Power drill

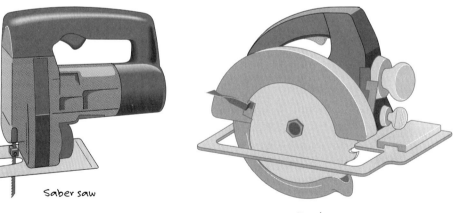

Saber saw

Circular saw

Adhesives

Because of my job, I travel a lot with my toolbox in hand, demonstrating projects on television and giving do-it-yourself seminars around the country. Once, when I was hurrying through an airport, the heel of my right shoe broke off. No problem! I just took out some superglue from my toolbox, glued it back on, and I was on my way.

Most glues need time to set before the repaired item is pressed into use. In fact, wood glue must always be clamped after it is applied. "C" clamps are ideal for many wood projects. Be sure to place a block of wood between the clamps and your project's surface to prevent damage. (Or you might want to look into buying "quick" clamps; most of them have rubber protectors on them.) Sometimes standard clamps just don't work. I've wrapped old panty hose around some projects to keep pieces together as the glue dries. Whatever you use, just be careful, you don't want to damage your project.

Now, back to the choice of the actual adhesive. While you may not have any spare superglue on you while hobbling through the airport—though it's not a bad idea—there are plenty of other times that you'll need the right adhesive as you're doing home projects. Here's a quick look at the different types that you'll want to keep close at hand.

WOOD GLUE   Wood glue may look like your children's classroom glue, but don't let looks deceive you. It's definitely not the same thing. Wood glue is designed to dry with a stronger bond than the wood itself. Use polyurethane or other weatherproof wood glue for outdoor projects.

EPOXY   When you don't know what adhesive to use, choose epoxy. This adhesive—a special mixture of resin and hardener—will bond almost any surface, and it's waterproof.

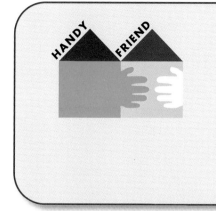

Karen Kalman from Dremel gives her best advice for how to enjoy your projects: "Before you launch into any project, make sure you have a genuine interest in what you're doing. For example, if you love to watch birds outside your window, start out by building a simple birdhouse. If you are a bookworm, design your own bookcase or wall shelf. Look for projects that combine passion, enjoyment, and personal satisfaction. Having passion for a project means you'll have the propensity and momentum to enjoy the process of working on the project—and not just finishing the project."

SEMISOLID EPOXY   This is great because it will even work on wet surfaces, so it's tailor-made for plumbing emergencies. The resin and the hardener are two different colors and will change to one color when they're properly mixed and ready to use.

SUPERGLUE OR CYANOACRYLATE-BASED ADHESIVES
Superglues are great for a quick, tight bond. However, don't use them on clear glass because ultraviolet rays will break down the bonding agent. For porous material or a vertical surface, use a gel superglue. To prevent what I call "glue run-on" or an unwanted trail of glue, look for gel superglue in special dispensers.

Simple Solution

When using superglue, keep a bottle of acetone-based fingernail polish remover handy just in case you get glue on your fingers.

The next time you're in your hardware store, take time to browse through the adhesive section. You'll see a lot more specialty products than the ones I've described. You don't need them for all projects but, sooner or later, you will. It's good to know what's available.

PLAY IT SAFE!

- Store your tools out of reach of children and pets.

- Resist using a screwdriver as a chisel or pry bar because that could damage the tip (and you) in the process.

- Similarly, don't use a wood chisel for anything other than mortising wood.

- Invest in safety goggles that fit your face securely.

- Always wear safety goggles when operating power tools, striking tools, and cutting tools and as recommended by manufacturers.

- Never begin a project when you are physically or mentally fatigued. Your fatigue could lead you to make costly and dangerous mistakes.

- To avoid sore thumbs, always keep your eye on the nail—not the hammer.

- When working with glue, paint, mineral spirits, or any substance containing fumes, make sure to keep your work area well ventilated.

"HandyMa'am®

with Beverly DeJulio"

A national public television show

You can make a lamp out of almost anything. Theme a lamp for the room or to reflect a special interest. See page 98.

Simply splice the wallpaper border when one piece isn't long enough to cover the area. See page 50.

You can save money and get creative by making your own candles. See page 96.

Recover your dining room chairs and watch the room come to life! See page 159.

Room screens can give privacy and add a display area. See page 149.

Whoever thought junk mail could look so good?! Recycling discarded paper makes a super, eco-friendly HandyFamily activity. See page 41.

Make a water fountain the focal point of a room or your private garden oasis. See page 175.

It's easy to install mitered corner tiles to the edge of your countertop. See page 106.

PVC pipes can be used to make many helpful items, like this desk organizer. Get the kids involved in this one. See page 163.

It's inexpensive and simple to give a new look to your kitchen. Just replace the center panel from one or more cabinet doors with beautiful colored glass. See page 111.

Use *faux* stained glass to create decorative windows, an original room divider, or a new look for your kitchen cabinet! See page 72.

Making a headboard is an easy carpentry project. They can be made out of many different materials and in just as many styles. See page 141.

Fiber rugs enhance the decor and add warmth to any room. See page 62.

Installing a tip-out tray in false drawer fronts adds handy storage.
See page 113.

Tin punch art is a constructive way for your kids to use up some of that excess energy and help you to decorate the home at the same time!
See page 12.

Add style and save money by making your own shower curtains out of colorful sheets.
See page 129.

Use glass blocks instead of glass to add a bit of privacy, while still allowing sunlight into the room.
See page 75.

Professional-looking brick walkways and patios are easier to install than you may think.
See page 172.

Color Your World

3

Painting and hanging wallcovering are the most common do-it-yourself projects. Why? Because in one fell swoop you can dramatically change the look of a room. Think about what your living room would look like if one wall were a completely different color from the rest. Think about the difference patterned wallpaper could make. The possibilities are as unlimited as your imagination.

The Walls around Us

When you think about it, we have it pretty easy when it comes to home-making. Before technology made homebuilding easier, people in earlier civilizations made their walls out of mud. As you can imagine, that was an extremely painstaking and time-consuming process. Now, most of our walls are made for us out of drywall, which manufacturers make from a combination of ground Gypsum rock and heavy paper. And you can get your drywall in all different sizes to meet your needs, though most of the time you're dealing with a 4 ft. × 8 ft. sheet from ½ to ⅝ of an inch thick. That's something helpful to know when it comes time to patch your walls.

Paint and Wallcovering Choices

With the development of prepasted wallcoverings and latex paint, many of us redo our walls often. Not long ago, we thought these jobs called for professionals.

Paints are a lot safer these days, too. Lead-free paint is much healthier for us, as are paints that do not contain any oil-based solvents. Those solvents known as volatile organic compounds (VOCs) can be hazardous to our health and they contribute to air pollution. The newer latex paints contain very little VOCs, and the best part of that is they are odor-free because it's the VOCs that contain those obnoxious-smelling fumes. Remember how badly you'd want to move out of your house anytime someone decided to paint even the smallest area?

Selecting a Paint Finish

Paints come in a variety of finishes, from flat at one end of the spectrum to hi-gloss at the other. These finishes vary in terms of the amount of light they reflect: I call this the shine factor. They also vary in another significant way: quality.

The old saying, "You get what you pay for!" certainly holds true when it comes to paint. There are so many variables that can affect the price of paint. So when you see paint at an unbelievably low price, beware—it may take three coats to achieve even coverage, driv-ing the overall cost of painting a room up. Price varies from manufacturer to manufacturer and as for "designer" paints, we all know you pay extra for the name!

The finish ("shine factor"), as well as whether it is oil or latex, or if enamel has been added, also will affect the price. In general, you'll find that flat or matte finishes are the least expensive. While you'll probably want to keep the relative prices of the different finishes in mind, don't let this drive your decision to the exclusion of two other key deciding factors: washability and durability. As you'll see below, these factors are directly variable with the level of light reflected by the paint. Once you determine the type of finish you need for the project at hand, then compare price and quality. Overall, I'd suggest that you invest in good quality paint, since it'll save you money and time in the long run.

Simple Solution

Proper paint disposal is very important. Dried latex paint can be disposed of through regular garbage pickup. Before throwing out latex paint, remove the lid and let the paint solidify. Oil-based paint should never be tossed into your regular trash. Instead, take it to a hazardous waste collection center for proper disposal. If you're not sure where to take it, call your local sanitation or health department.

FLAT A flat finish, as you might imagine, doesn't have any shine at all. It is primarily used on interior walls and ceilings for a traditional matte look. Because it does not shine, imperfections are less visible. Flat paint is not a good choice for walls that need to be cleaned often (such as kitchen walls) as it will not sustain repeated washings.

EGGSHELL Eggshell also helps to hide small imperfections because it does not reflect much light, although it has a bit more shine than matte. It is also slightly more washable than matte, making it a good choice for a teenager's bedroom.

SATIN This finish can be a good choice if you want the look of matte, the durability of a semigloss, and just a hint of sheen. Just like satin fabric, this paint does not appear to have a sheen when you look at it straight on but, from an angle, it looks like a semigloss finish. A satin finish can withstand washings with a mild detergent, making it a good candidate for a "high traffic" room (for example, the den or a young child's bedroom).

SEMIGLOSS Interior trim, furniture, kitchens, and bathrooms are traditionally painted with semigloss paint for a surface that reflects light and is highly washable. Word to the wise: only use a semigloss finish on smooth surfaces because it will not hide imperfections.

GLOSS AND HI-GLOSS For a high shine on doors, furniture, metal surfaces, and any items that are put to the test everyday, many people choose gloss or hi-gloss paint. Now, once painted, every surface flaw will reflect back at you, so try to minimize and eliminate every imperfection before you pick up that paintbrush or spray can!

ADDING ENAMEL Manufacturers can add enamel to either latex or oil paint to improve durability and to make it easier to clean. Enamel helps paint dry to a harder finish, making it a perfect choice for surfaces subject to a lot of abuse. As you might have guessed, a hi-gloss paint with enamel added would have the toughest finish of all, making it ideal for surfaces that have to stand up to the elements (such as kitchen cabinets and furniture).

Preparing a Wall for Painting and Wallcoverings

The most important step in painting and hanging wallcovering is wall preparation. Don't depend on paint or wallpaper to fill or cover cracks, nail holes, and other minor wall damage. Also, if there's old wallcovering on the walls, remove it. Take the time to do it right!

Before we start, let's talk about how to keep the kids occupied while you're busy changing the look of your walls.

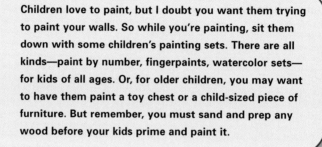

Children love to paint, but I doubt you want them trying to paint your walls. So while you're painting, sit them down with some children's painting sets. There are all kinds—paint by number, fingerpaints, watercolor sets—for kids of all ages. Or, for older children, you may want to have them paint a toy chest or a child-sized piece of furniture. But remember, you must sand and prep any wood before your kids prime and paint it.

How to Strip Wallpaper and Other Wallcoverings

You really shouldn't paint or apply new wallcovering over existing wallcovering. Seams from old wallpaper will show through and the extra weight can weaken the old adhesive, causing it to come loose. Also, before you start cover your floors and any furniture that cannot be removed from the room where you are working with plastic drop cloths or newspaper.

● Removing Wallpaper That Has No Coating (such as vinyl or paint)

WHAT YOU NEED **Stripper**   **Putty or broad knife**
Sprayer, sponge, or roller

STEP 1   Apply a commercial wallpaper stripper to the existing wallpaper. Most are concentrates, so add water per manufacturer's guidelines or try one of the newer gel removers. Also, try to use a stripper with enzymes because they attack the adhesive and break it down, making it faster and easier to remove the paper. Apply the stripper to about four strips at a time, using either a sprayer or sponge for liquid stripper or a roller for gel.

Simple Solution

If any area gets too difficult to remove, just add more stripper.

STEP 2   Start removing the paper at the top with a putty knife or broad knife and scrape gently. Be careful; if you scrape too hard you may damage your wall!

● Removing Several Layers of Wallcovering, Wallcovering That's Been Painted Over, or Coated Wallcovering

WHAT YOU NEED   **Scoring tool** (Paper Tiger recommended)
Stripper
Sprayer, sponge, or roller
Putty or broad knife

STEP 1   Using a scoring tool, score through the layers so the stripper can get to the adhesive.

STEP 2   Apply the stripper and remove with putty or broad knife.

Simple Solution

Once all the paper is removed, remove any adhesive residue that's been left behind. Dilute your stripper and just wash the walls with it. Rinse with fresh water. Some areas may need to be sanded.

● Removing Strippable Wallcovering

WHAT YOU NEED   **Putty or broad knife**   **Stripper**
Sprayer, sponge, or roller

STEP 1   Loosen the bottoms of the strips of wallcovering with a putty or broad knife.

STEP 2   Gently pull the paper off from the loose ends. If it does not come off easily, apply stripping solution.

STEP 3   Most strippable wallcovering will leave a paper or fabric mesh backing on the wall. Remove it by using stripping solution and by following directions for removing wallpaper that has no coating.

● Removing Wallpaper Using a Steamer

Another way to remove wallpaper is with a steam machine. It looks a lot like an iron with a much larger reservoir. Basically, steam coming from holes in the sole plate softens the adhesive so it can be scraped away.

But let me tell you a little story before you go the steamer route. When my fourth child, Angel, was just a few weeks old I decided to change the paper in our upstairs bathroom. But I found that every time I used a putty knife to scrap the paper off, I removed not only the paper but some drywall as well. So, I decided to rent a steamer for this stubborn paper. It was only after I spent several hours perched on a ladder sweating it out in the middle of a hot and humid summer day that I decided steamers should be used only in the winter. There was some good news, though. I lost the ten pounds of pregnancy weight working in that "steamed" bathroom, and my skin looked great for days afterwards.

How to Patch Up Holes and Cracks

WHAT YOU NEED   Spackling paste
Putty knife
Fine-grade sandpaper
Sanding block
Drywall screws

For larger holes:
Drywall
Drywall or keyhole saw
Wooden strips (paint stirrers)
Drywall screws
Pencil
Fiberglass drywall tape (self-adhesive)

● Patching Small Holes and Cracks

STEP 1   Make sure the areas around all holes and cracks are clean and dust free. Also, remove any loose material such as paint or old spackle.

STEP 2   Press spackling paste into cracks and holes with a putty knife. Overfill the area slightly and let it dry. See manufacturer's guidelines for drying times.

STEP 3   When the paste is dry, sand it to a smooth finish with a fine-grade sandpaper and a sanding block.

STEP 4   If any of the nails holding the drywall to the studs have popped out, they need to be removed or driven entirely back into the studs.

Place a nail set in the middle of the popped nail head and hammer the nail back into the stud. This will cause the least amount of damage, leaving just a small hole in the wallboard.

STEP 5   Secure the wallboard now by installing wallboard screws within 2 or 3 in. above and below the popped nail.

STEP 6   Overfill both the recessed screws and popped nail head areas with spackling putty.

STEP 7   Let the putty dry and sand smooth.

Simple Solution

After cleaning up the area around holes and cracks, wipe it with a paintbrush to make sure it's dust free.

Simple Solution

Tighten the wallboard screw so it goes slightly past the wall's surface (think of it as a "dimple" in the wall). Just don't screw it in so deep that it breaks through the wallboard's protective paper covering.

Simple Solution

If you need to fill some nail holes but don't have putty, mix some cornstarch with water until you have a smooth paste. You can use your "cornstarch putty" to fill in those small nail holes.

● How to Patch Large Holes

STEP 1   Cut a square patch of drywall (make sure it's the same thickness as your wall) slightly larger than the hole in your wall. Cutting drywall is easy. Just score the drywall with a utility knife and snap it.

STEP 2   Place the patch over the damaged area and trace around it with a pencil. Make a mark at the top of the patch so you will know which way it goes when you install it.

STEP 3   Check inside the wall for pipes and wires using a small mirror and a flashlight to guide your search.

STEP 4   Use a drywall or keyhole saw and cut out the damaged area along the pencil mark. If there are wires or pipes in the way or if you're not sure of their exact location, keep the saw's cuts shallow, in order not to disturb anything.

STEP 5   The patch will need a secure backing—otherwise, it will fall between the walls. Insert wooden strips (one-by-twos or even paint stirrers)—they should be about 4 in. longer than the opening—in the opening and use one hand to keep them against the back of the wall. Secure in place with a drywall screw on each end.

> ## Simple Solution
>
> **All patched areas should be primed before painting or hanging wallcovering. The patching compound is very porous when it dries. If you don't prime to seal it, the paint will be absorbed differently and dry a different shade than the surrounding painted surfaces. With wallcovering adhesive, the glue will be absorbed, causing the wallpaper to come loose.**

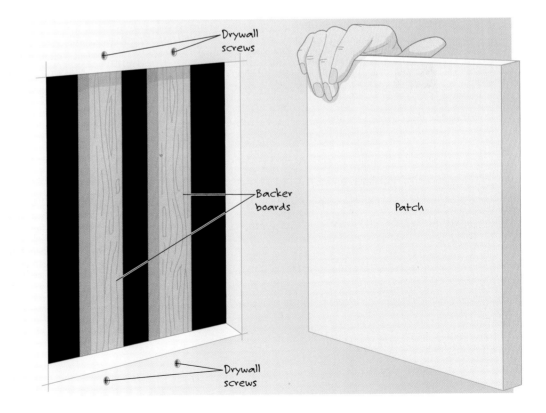

Drywall screws

Backer boards

Patch

Drywall screws

STEP 6 Put the patch into place and secure with drywall screws.

STEP 7 Cover the seams with self-sticking fiberglass drywall tape, which I think is the easiest to work with. Don't let the tape overlap because this will cause a bump in your wall.

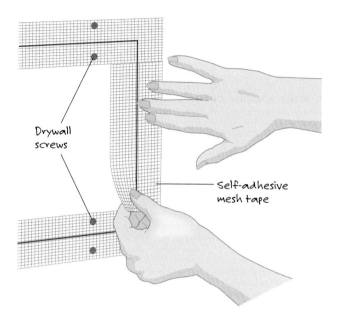

Drywall screws

Self-adhesive mesh tape

STEP 8 Apply one or two coats of patching compound. Allow the compound to dry in between each layer (see manufacturer's guidelines on drying time). For each layer, you want to cover an area slightly larger than the previous layer. Sand in between each application.

Cleaning Walls

Once your patches are taken care of, you want to make sure your surface is clean and dry before you paint or hang wallcovering. In most rooms, wash the walls using a mild detergent and rinse. In the kitchen, however, you may need to use a degreaser. TSP (trisodium phosphate), a powder that mixes with water, works well and will also help degloss shiny paint (gloss and semigloss finishes). It's difficult for adhesive or paint to make a secure bond on a slick surface.

Simple Solution

Stains on walls, such as water marks, need to be primed and sealed to prevent them from "bleeding" through fresh paint or wallcovering.

Paint Applicators

There are several ways to apply paint. The most popular tools are rollers and brushes, but I've used everything from a sponge to a rag to a cotton swab or cosmetic sponge (for touch-ups).

ROLLERS   There are several rollers to choose from. They vary in terms of the fabric covering the roller (like floor carpeting, it ranges from short nap to long) and the length of the handle. Think about what you're going to be painting and check your paint manufacturer's guidelines before choosing the roller nap for your project. In general, you'll select a short nap for smooth surfaces and longer naps for rough ones (such as stucco).

BRUSHES   Several types of brushes are available. There are natural and synthetic bristle brushes and ones made of foam. In general, use natural for oil-based paints and synthetic for either oil-based or latex. You can use foam for all types of paint. The tips of the bristles should be chiseled (tapered) and flagged (split). We don't want split ends on our hair, but it's good for paint brushes.

How to Paint Your Walls

Before you start working with your primer and paints, cover floors with drop cloths or newspapers. I prefer heavy-duty canvas or plastic drop cloths, because paint more easily seeps through newspaper. When possible, move whatever furniture you can out of the room. And, as previously suggested, if you can't remove it, cover it!

Next, before you forget, write down the brand, color name, and number of the paint you'll be using, in case you need to buy more in the middle of the project and paint has dribbled and dried on top of that information (it happens) or for future repairs. In fact, assemble paint chips to record the paints used throughout your house. Because the paper chips are so small, I keep the paint stirrers, drill a hole in the end of each, and thread twine through the holes. On each stirrer, I write the color, brand, and what I used it on. Believe me, this will save you plenty of grief when you try to remember all those various colors you have in the house. And keep your "color boards" with your paint supplies for easy access.

STEP 1 Before applying paint, of course, make sure walls are smooth, clean, and dry; prime over any newly installed drywall, patches, and stained areas.

STEP 2 Have the store mix the paint on its machines and then stir the paint right before using it, as paint separates when it sits. If you have had the paint sitting for a while, try your best to start preparing it about a day before using it. Shake and turn the can upside down and let it sit for 24 hours, then stir thoroughly.

STEP 3 If you have a variable-speed drill, you can use a special propeller-like attachment on your drill to mix the paint. Be careful; make sure to use the low speed (or you'll have a splatter effect on your walls, whether you want it or not).

STEP 4 Pour paint from the large can to a smaller container. If you're using a roller, pour the paint into the roller tray, but don't pour so much that it starts to cover the ridged part of the tray.

STEP 5 Close the can. This keeps the can from drying out, picking up dirt and grime, or spilling. I'll never forget the time I was painting my bathroom and I realized that there was a fly in my nice yellow paint.

Simple Solution

Before choosing a paint, discuss your concerns with an informed salesperson. There are special paints formulated for specific needs. For example, you should paint your kitchen or bathroom (or greenhouse, if you have one) with moisture- and mildew-resistant paints. The paint won't peel in humid conditions.

Simple Solution

Always paint *into* freshly painted areas to help prevent lap marks.

There is an order to painting that will make life easier. Start at the top of a room first, leaving for last the trims and moldings (follow the order: ceiling, walls, crown moldings, chair rails, then around doors and windows, and, finally, base molding). The reason for doing walls and ceiling before moldings is that it is easier to put masking tape on a flat surface (i.e., walls) than on a curved one. Just be sure that wall and ceiling paint is dry before taping, and use low-tack painter's tape. To prevent disappointment, remove the tape *before* paint dries; otherwise it will pull some of the dried paint off with it. Remove or mask off anything you don't want to get paint on (i.e., door hinges, switches, and outlets—turn off power and remove plates to mask over switches and outlets).

Simple Solution

To protect against paint splatters and drips, use masking tape that has a plastic film attached to it to cover vanities and medicine cabinets, and tie large plastic bags around chandeliers, ceiling fans, and lighting fixtures.

● Painting with a Roller

Before using a roller, use a brush for what's called "cutting in." All that means is painting the areas that are hard to get to with a roller, such as corners and around doors, windows, and moldings.

STEP 1 Work in an area about 3 ft. × 4 ft., which is about the coverage of a single roller-load of paint. Load your roller; roll it over the ridges of the tray to get rid of excess. Don't roll too fast—you don't want the paint to splatter!

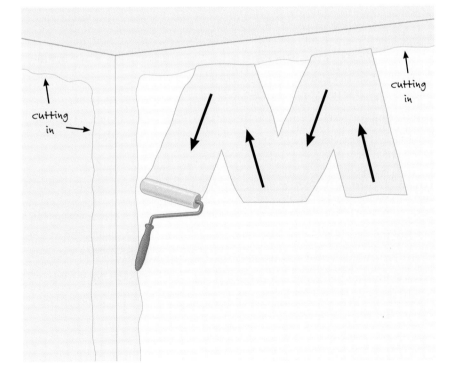

cutting in →

cutting in

cutting in

STEP 2 Without lifting the roller off the wall, start by making an "M" and then roll horizontally, back and forth across the "M." This will roll the paint on evenly. (The "M" will be backwards if you paint from left to right, because you should always start away from freshly painted areas, rolling into them as you apply the paint.)

STEP 3 For walls, start painting at the ceiling in 3 ft. × 4 ft. sections and work your way down.

STEP 4 After you finish a 4 ft.-wide area, make a continuous stroke from top to bottom (ceiling to floor) to even out the paint and eliminate roller marks.

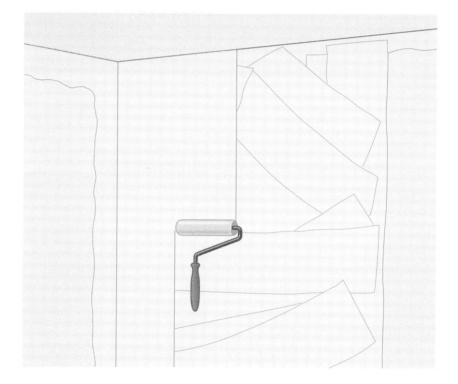

STEP 5 Let the first layer dry before applying a second coat, if needed.

Basic Spray Painting

In the mood for instant gratification? Get a can of spray paint and let your imagination run wild!

Spray painting is a quick and easy way to get creative. If you haven't checked out the spray paints that are now available, you will find the options stunning. You can improve the look of practically anything with different techniques such as stenciling and applying specialty finishes. Tired of that *faux* brass finish on your bed frame? Get a can of instant crackle finish or marble spray paint and give your bed a much more sophisticated look.

As with any other painting project, the surface should be prepared first. Spray painting should always be done in a well-ventilated area. And to avoid the messiness of spray painting, make a spray booth to hold the overspray. Cut one side out of a large cardboard box and place the item to be painted inside.

And, of course, remember to use a back-and-forth motion while spraying. Move your entire arm back and forth, not just your wrist!

Simple Solution

It's easy to keep your new walls from getting scratched by pictures or any other wall hangings. Put peel-and-stick felt pads on the back side corners of the wall hangings. Or squeeze a bead of silicone adhesive on the corners. When the adhesive is cured, it's a rubbery material that will protect your walls, and it keeps the picture hanging straight.

Camouflage That Wall

In homes with plaster walls and ceilings, harmless imperfections may be visible on the interior surfaces. These dimples and depressions are really just cosmetic, so it's hard to make an argument for paying big bucks to replaster or install drywall over the old walls. One way to make these problem walls and ceilings look better is to apply a textured paint. You can even use these techniques to give new life to old, scuffed wood paneling.

ADDING TEXTURE   You can ask the paint dealer to add texture to any paint color you chose. Or, if you'd rather do it yourself, you can buy powdered additives in fine, medium, or coarse grit. Check the label of the additive product for the type of applicator recommended.

Generally, you'll see a loop roller recommended as the best tool for spreading thicker texture evenly on the wall's surface, with a regular paintbrush reserved for those areas that need to be cut in. However, you do not have to feel limited to these choices. Many have experimented successfully with an array of tools to apply textured paint—such as combs, serrated trowels, or broad knives. Depending on the tool selected, you can achieve a variety of effects from swirls and waves to adobe textures.

FAUX **FINISHES**   Another way to fool the eye and keep it from noticing flawed surfaces is by using *trompe l'oeil* or *faux* finish paint techniques like marbleizing, sponging, and rag-rolling (ragging).

All those fancy finishes you've seen in magazines or in designer show rooms really boil down to just two simple painting methods: positive painting, which is applying a glaze to a painted wall, or negative painting, which is removing wet glaze off a finished surface.

Sponging and ragging are the most common methods of positive painting. Applying a special paint glaze with a sea sponge gives a soft, impressionistic effect. Applying the glaze with rags, crinkled paper, or bunched-up cellophane or plastic wrap is much more dramatic. Using these application techniques, the glaze makes bold veins of color across the walls.

Negative painting is sometimes called *combing* because hard combs are a popular choice for scraping patterns of fine lines into paint glaze. But any number of removers can be used, from rags and crumpled paper and cellophane to a stippling brush, cotton swabs, and toothbrushes. Cut "teeth" in a rubber squeegee and use to slice a pattern into the wet glaze. Or you can do a large room in a hurry by taking a big plastic drop cloth and squishing it around on a freshly glazed wall.

Removing paint glaze from a surface for negative painting techniques requires working quickly because the glaze must be removed before it dries. Because it takes longer to dry, oil-based glaze is a little easier to work with than latex. Incidentally, you can apply oil-based glazes over oil or latex base coats, but a latex-based glaze does not adhere well to an oil paint base coat.

You make a glaze with a blend of paint and solvent or you can buy glazing liquid and add it to the paint of your choice. Follow the instructions that come with the glaze. Feel free to experiment, because the consistency of the thinned paint is really a matter of personal preference. Just be sure to jot down instructions when you get the consistency you like so it can be recreated. And remember, there really is no right or wrong way when it comes to these different *faux* finish techniques. If you do something and make a so-called mistake but still love the results, keep it. It's your home. You're the only one who has to truly love it. And if the day comes that *you* don't like it anymore, you can just paint over it!

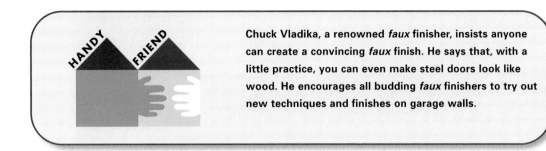

Chuck Vladika, a renowned *faux* finisher, insists anyone can create a convincing *faux* finish. He says that, with a little practice, you can even make steel doors look like wood. He encourages all budding *faux* finishers to try out new techniques and finishes on garage walls.

WAINSCOTING   Here's another way that you can hide some of your walls. Actually wainscoting, which is the term for any wood wallcovering that extends from the height of a chair rail down to the floor, is often just used for its decorative value. Originally, when it first came into use in the 1500s, it was created to block drafts that came through the walls. In any case, wainscoting varies in appearance from simple wood paneling to custom-made carved pieces with intricate detailing.

Not long ago, installing raised panel wainscoting was a job relegated to professionals, but now there are easy-to-use kits available. The manufacturer includes all the parts and assembly is like putting together a puzzle.

The most important part of wainscoting is making sure it's perfectly level. You'll want to install it about a quarter of an inch above the floor and trim it with a shoe molding. And as with most wood applications on walls, you'll be using construction adhesive and finishing nails to attach it.

Most of these kits come with unfinished wood. I always stain before hanging; however, if I decide to paint, I do it after installation because the paint buildup will make it harder to fit the pieces together.

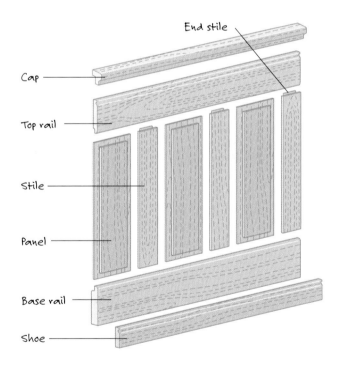

End stile

Cap

Top rail

Stile

Panel

Base rail

Shoe

Paper It!

You'll probably find that you prefer wallpaper for some rooms in your home. The first time that I tackled wallpapering completely on my own was when I decorated my daughter Christine's room in our first house. Vince was four and Christine was two and they had shared a room decorated in red, white, and blue. For Christine's new room of her very own, I decided to do the pink thing.

I promptly went out and found some beautiful pink floral paper and bought *most* of the supplies the clerk recommended, but I cut a few corners. For instance, I decided to make my own plumb line with a string, a thumbtack, a washer, and the kids' chalk. And I was certain I didn't need the water tray because I planned to dip the wallpaper in the bathtub.

Well, it took me a while to finally get up the nerve to cut the first strip, which I then rolled up and submerged in the tub. When it was ready to be taken out, I was not prepared for how much excess water there was. It was still dripping as I hurried down the hall, dripping water on the hallway carpet. I ran across the bedroom to the back wall leaving a trail of water and wallpaper paste.

That was the only trip I made from tub to wall. My next trip was to the store to purchase one of those handy-dandy water trays, which I quickly set up on the long folding table that we keep for arts and craft and Thanksgiving dinner. With the paper soaking right at my side, I could stop worrying about getting water all over the house.

Now, before we get you started off on the *right* foot with your wallpapering project, why not have the kids make their own paper (although this paper is *not* suitable for wallpapering)? This handmade paper can be used for place cards, stationery, gift tags, and invitations, and is a great way to recycle junk mail.

Recycle all that scrap paper from around the house—notebook paper, bond, newspapers, and that unwanted junk mail (but not glossy paper like magazines!). First, tear it into small pieces—kids love ripping paper—then soak it in water, blend it all together (yes, in a regular blender), shape it on framed screens, and let it dry. If you want to dye the paper, add fabric dye or tea leaves while it's soaking. There are plenty of paper-making books and kits at your local craft store to get you started. Once they've got the paper made, your kids can use it to create their very own party invitations, greeting cards, and stationery. For my daughter's engagement party, we made the invitations, and later I surprised everyone with some of our family's favorite recipes printed on homemade recipe cards.

How to Hang Wallpaper

WHAT YOU NEED

Wallpaper (How much depends on the size of the area you're covering; remember to measure twice!)
Water tray
Scissors
Broad knife or straightedge

Pencil
Utility knife
Tape measure
Clean sponges/rags
Stepladder (if needed)
Plumb line/level
Thumbtacks

Remember those old comedy shows like *I Love Lucy,* when the characters had so much trouble hanging wallpaper? In no time flat, they'd be covered with glue, wallpaper was wrapped all around them, and crooked paper was hanging from the walls. Well, there's no reason to let that scare you. In fact, hanging wallcovering is becoming one of the most popular do-it-yourself decorating projects. With all the new advances—such as improved prepasted and strippable paper—it's a project that's well within reach for beginners. And the different textures, patterns, and colors always bring out the hidden designer in all of us.

But like all home projects, have patience and pay attention to detail. Use high-quality products and allow plenty of time to do your job. Like me, I'm sure you want to see results as soon as possible, but taking that extra time means a lot more enjoyment of your work in the long run.

STEP 1 Prepare walls by patching holes and cracks.

STEP 2 Make sure the surface to be covered is clean, dry, and smooth.

STEP 3 Paint any areas that come in contact with the surface being covered—like ceilings, moldings, and window and door frames—before applying wallcovering.

STEP 4 Apply a primer/sizer. You may be tempted to skip this step, but don't! There are three major benefits:

- It allows you to slide the covering on the wall instead of having to pull it off to reposition it.

- It makes a stronger bond between the paper and the wall.

- It makes it easier to remove the paper when you decided you want to change the look of the room.

So, the primer/sizer has benefits when the paper is hung, when the paper is hanging, and when it's time to take it off!

STEP 5 Measure the width of your paper strip and subtract ½ in. Now, near the top of the wall, measure this distance out from the corner and mark with a pencil. (Don't use a pen, because it may bleed through the paper later on!)

STEP 6 Drop what's called a plumb line along this pencil mark. (Basically, a plumb line is a vertical line perpendicular to the floor that is used as a guideline for hanging your first strip.) Tack a chalk-coated string at the pencil mark, tie a weight at the bottom of the string, let the weight stop moving, allow the string to rest against the wall. Pull down on the weight, hold tight, and snap the string by pulling it away from the wall a couple of inches and letting go quickly (to get an impression of the chalk on the wall) and then remove the string. And, you've got a plumb line! Or, use a pencil, a level, and a straightedge to draw a plumb line. Place the straightedge on the pencil mark, check to see that it is plumb using the level, and draw a vertical line.

Simple Solution

If you are covering all the walls in a room, start in a hidden area, like behind a door or big wall unit. It should be a spot you don't notice when you first walk into a room, because as you work your way around the room, chances are you're going to have a mismatched pattern at that last corner. You want to make it as unnoticeable as possible.

Simple Solution

Wall and ceiling joints are not perfectly straight, so make sure you drop a new plumb line every time you turn a corner.

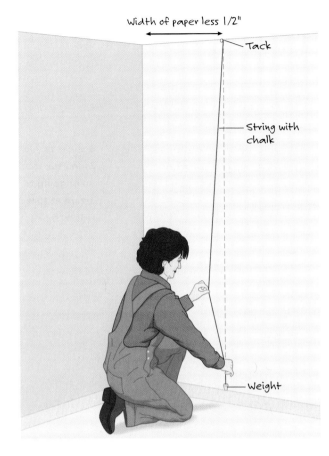

STEP 7 Cut strips of paper 6 in. longer than the wall height in order to leave three inches of overhang at the top and bottom of the wall. The excess paper allows for unevenness of walls and ceilings. Match the pattern of each new strip to the previous strip.

STEP 8 If I cut several strips at a time, I number the strips, as I cut them, on the top backside of the paper with a pencil. This will ensure that you hang them in the right order so the pattern matches up correctly.

STEP 9 Wet prepasted paper by rolling the paper from bottom to top with the pattern on the inside. Place the paper in the water tray, gently pushing to get rid of air bubbles, and leave it in there according to the time recommended by the manufacturer.

STEP 10 Slowly draw the paper out of the water tray, making sure the adhesive backing is wet.

STEP 11 Now, book the paper. Simply fold the bottom of the paper to the middle (adhesive inside) and the top to the middle (like a book!). Do *not* crease the paper. The reason you book the paper is that, when you put the paper into water, it expands unevenly and will spread at the seams if you hang it immediately. Booking it allows it to stabilize and the adhesive to get activated. Follow manufacturer's directions for how long you should book your strips.

STEP 12 Now you're ready to hang your first strip. Unbook the top half and remember to leave that three inches on top and line the edge of the paper with the plumb line, sliding it into place. Do *not* pull it into place because this can damage the paper.

STEP 13 Smooth out the paper using a smoothing tool. Start from the center of the paper moving up and down—then smooth out toward the sides. This eliminates those nasty air bubbles.

STEP 14 Trim off that excess paper using a straightedge and a utility knife. (I like the type with snap-off blade tips for this project; a sharp blade is essential when trimming wallcovering.) Rinse the ceiling with a sponge to clean off any adhesive that may have gotten on it from the excess trim.

STEP 15 Unfold the bottom half of the paper and smooth it onto the wall, again lining it up with the plumb line.

STEP 16 Trim the corner and bottom excess and wipe clean any surface such as the base molding or floor, where adhesive may have spread.

STEP 17 Rinse the wallcovering with a sponge again to make sure there is no adhesive residue on the paper.

STEP 18 Remembering to book each strip, hang the top of the next strip first and place it as close to the first strip as possible. Use both hands to slide the strip into place. Make sure to match up the pattern.

STEP 19 Smooth, trim, and rinse just as you did with the first strip, and continue doing the same until the entire surface is covered.

STEP 20 After the paper has been up for 15 minutes, you want to lightly roll seams using a seam roller. Don't push down on the roller too hard. If you do, adhesive will squeeze out and the seams may eventually come loose.

Simple Solution

When you pick up your rolls of wallcovering, check to see if they have the same "run" number. This means they were all printed at the factory on the same day and that the dye will be the exact same in every roll. You should also write down the run number and file it just in case you need more paper in the future.

Simple Solution

Change the water in the water tray often so you don't have water mixed with adhesive that may have come off the paper when you were wetting it.

Get It Cornered

In a perfect world, the width of your wall covering would be such that it would fit perfectly so that you wouldn't have to deal with cutting and trimming for corners. (And there wouldn't be any laundry or parking tickets or . . . but I digress.) Anyway, since most of us don't live in a perfect world, this section is going to give you the steps you'll need to finesse wallpapering corners. The most important ingredient for success: patience. (If you have any issues with perfectionism, this is a great opportunity to work on them!)

SCENARIO 1 **You approach the corner of the room and the amount of wallcovering to be "wrapped" into (inside the corner) or around (outside the corner) a corner is 2 in. or less.** In this case, go ahead, "wrap" the corner and drop a new plumb line (to determine exactly where that plumb line gets dropped: measure the width of your wallcovering, subtract ¼ in., then measure that distance from the edge of the wrapped paper) for the first full strip of wallpaper on the next wall. There will be a little overlap once the new piece is positioned against the plumb line.

SCENARIO 2 **The amount of paper to be "wrapped" into an inside corner exceeds 2 in.** In this case, measure from the edge of the last full strip to the corner in at least three places—at the top, middle, and bottom of the wall—and then add ¼ in. to the widest measurement. Measure out this amount on the next piece of wallpaper you plan to hang and mark it with a line running along its entire length. (Remember to measure from the pattern side that matches the pattern sequence of the piece hanging on the wall.) Cut along the line—your original full strip of wallpaper is now in two strips. Apply the measured side to the wall, matching the pattern— it should wrap the corner and extend onto the next wall slightly. After trimming the top and bottom of the wallpaper and rinsing off excess adhesive, you're going to trim the edge of the newly hung paper so that there's only ¹⁄₁₆ in. wrapping the corner. Use a straightedge or broad knife with the edge of the blade in the corner, trimming from the side of the blade where the excess paper is.

Measure the width of the leftover piece from the strip just applied, subtract ¼ in. and drop a plumb line at that measurement. Measure in several places from the corner to the plumb line to make sure that the cut piece of wallpaper will be wide enough to cover the wall all the way into the corner. If it comes up short at any point, move the plumb line closer to the corner.

Simple Solution

Before you begin wallpapering a room, buy a can of paint in a shade that closely matches the predominant background color of your wall covering. Before you start papering, and after the walls have been otherwise prepped for the new wall treatment, use this paint to paint a wide swath (say 3 in. wide) at each corner of the room. If you paint the corners to match the background of the paper, it saves you the hassle of trimming the strips individually when cornering the room. Instead, you can slice through both layers at the same time and the small gap of painted wall will blend in.

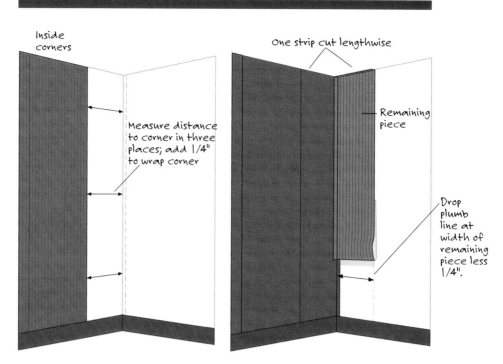

Inside corners

Measure distance to corner in three places; add 1/4" to wrap corner

One strip cut lengthwise

Remaining piece

Drop plumb line at width of remaining piece less 1/4".

Hang this second portion—following the plumb line and matching the pattern as best as possible—it will be a little off. Smooth, trim, and rinse off excess adhesive. Then pull the edge of the first strip away from the wall in the corner and allow the new strip to wrap into the corner. Trim off the excess of the leftover strip, so that it'll lap under the first piece by only about 1/16 in., then smooth the first strip back down. Use a special vinyl-to-vinyl adhesive here and wherever you have paper overlapping.

SCENARIO 3 **The amount of paper that'll wrap around an outside corner is more than 2 in.** First, measure from the edge of the last full strip to the corner at the top, middle, and bottom. Add 1 in. to the widest measurement. Use that measurement and make a line the entire length of the next strip of paper. (Measure from the side of the new strip that matches the pattern of the paper on the wall.) Cut along this line.

Hang this partial strip, then trim the top and bottom and rinse the paper as you have done with previous strips. Then use the width measurement of the leftover portion and add 3/4 in. to determine where to drop a plumb line on the next wall. From the new plumb line, measure at the top, middle, and bottom to the edge of the wallpaper strip that wrapped around the corner. Make sure the leftover portion of the strip will meet the first portion of the strip. In most places, it will overlap by about 1/4 in.

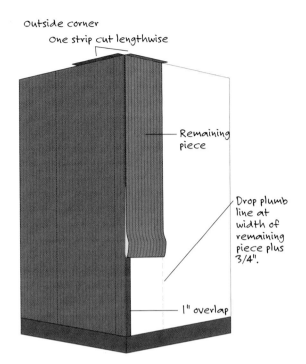

Outside corner

One strip cut lengthwise

Remaining piece

Drop plumb line at width of remaining piece plus 3/4".

1" overlap

Hang the leftover strip, lining up the edges with the plumb line and lining up the pattern as best you can. The pattern will not match perfectly because of the slight overlap.

Apply special vinyl-to-vinyl adhesive to areas that overlap or, using a straightedge to guide you, cut through the overlap and remove the trimmed pieces.

Papering around Outlets and Switches

Obviously, you may encounter some outlets and switches as you're covering your wall. No sweat! First, turn off the electricity at the fuse box or circuit breaker. Then remove the cover plates. Next, just hang the wallcovering over the outlets and switches, but don't smooth out the paper just yet. Using a utility knife, cut an "X," from corner to corner of the electrical box, to allow the wallcovering to relax around the obstacle. (Feel with your hand for the shape of the electrical device so you will know exactly where to make your "X.") Smooth the paper as usual; then using scissors, trim away the "X" so that it reveals the switch or outlet. (If your trim isn't perfect, don't worry: the outlet and switch plates will help you to fudge it.)

Around Doors and Windows

Just hang your paper, but immediately trim excess paper that's running over the window and door openings, leaving about two inches of excess overhang.

Using scissors, cut the wallpaper at an angle into the corner of the window or door trim.

Next, make a couple of cuts on each side of the angle cut. This will allow the paper to relax and go against the wall smoothly.

Smooth into place, trim, and wipe off any adhesive.

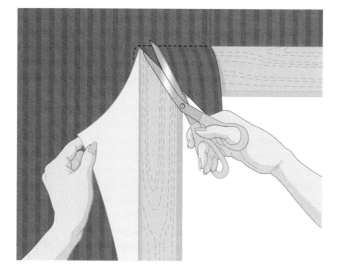

How to Hang Wallpaper Borders

WHAT YOU NEED Level/straightedge combination Pencil
Sponge or paint roller or paint brush Tape measure
Primer/sizer Water tray
Utility knife Straightedge or broad knife
Border

Many times you'll find that paint isn't quite enough to spruce up a room, while wallpaper might be too much. You might consider compromising with a wallpaper border. It's fast, easy to do, rather inexpensive, and best of all, it can add some real pizzazz to a plain wall.

Determining where the border is to be applied is your first choice. Use your imagination. I've seen them at chair rail height, eye level, as trim around doors and windows, at the top of the wall (like crown molding), and even at floor level in a children's room. Some folks even give borders a three-dimensional look by installing molding on either side.

STEP 1 Using a level, draw a level line across the wall at the height where you wish the border to be. If it will hang at or below eye level, draw the level line at the point where the bottom of the border will rest. If the border is above eye level, draw the line where the top of the border will be positioned so that any uncovered pencil mark is less visible.

STEP 2 Cut a sponge about $\frac{1}{4}$ in. shorter than the width of the border and use it to apply the primer/sizer. A short-napped paint roller slightly smaller than the width of the border can also be used to roll the primer/sizer on.

STEP 3 Measure the length of wall or area to be covered, add at least an inch, and cut the border to that length.

STEP 4 If you are hanging a border over vinyl-coated wall covering, even if the border is prepasted, apply a vinyl-to-vinyl adhesive following manufacturer's instructions. If a prepasted border is going up over bare wall, dip the border in water for the recommended time. Book it by gently folding it back and forth, like ribbon candy, with the paste sides touching. Be careful, however, not to crease the paper.

STEP 5 Hold the folded border in one hand and begin placing it on the wall with the other, following the pencil line you drew earlier. Work in the direction that is most comfortable for you, placing and smoothing the border using a sponge as you slide it into place.

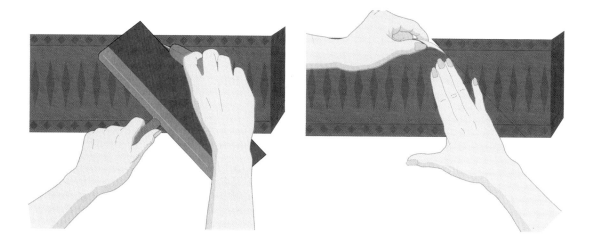

STEP 6 If you need to use more than one piece of paper along a wall to complete your border, overlap the two pieces, matching the pattern, and, using a straightedge and utility knife, cut through both layers at a 45-degree angle to make the seam less obvious. Remove the trimmed pieces after making the cut. Use a straightedge and utility knife to trim the ends of the border in the corners of the room.

STEP 7 Rinse off excess adhesive as soon as possible after hanging the border to prevent staining the border or the wall.

Bordering Doors and Windows

When applying a border around doors and windows, it's possible to achieve the appearance of a seamless run. Cut the border for the first side several inches longer than the length of the side being covered with the border, so that it's long enough to completely overlap the piece on the next side. Cut the border the width of the border plus 1 in. for each corner it will come in contact with. (For example: if your border is 4 in. wide, cut your border 5 in. longer for each corner that piece will be a part of; i.e., if you are cutting a piece to go along the side of a door you would only add an extra 5 in. to the length; if going across the top of a door you would add 10 in. to your measurement.) Apply this piece.

For the next side, hold the border at the corner where it will be placed—to get a match, turn the edge of the border at a 45-degree angle and keep moving this angle along the border until there's a good pattern continuation from the preceding strip of border. The pattern won't match perfectly. However, it will appear as though the pattern is continuing around the corner. (Not all patterns work well for this type of installation.)

Measure for this piece starting at the overlap—I usually just hold the border on the wall as I unroll it the distance needed (allowing for the overlap of the next piece—1 in. plus the width of the border). Cut and apply the border, overlapping the first piece by 1 in.

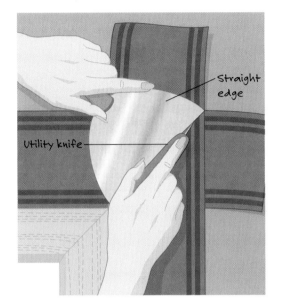

Hold a straightedge with one end of it at the casing corner and the other end at the outer edge of the intersecting borders, so you're forming a 45-degree angle. Then cut through both layers of the border using a utility knife.

Peel the ends of the border back and remove the cut, excess pieces of border.

Smooth the border back in place, line up the edges and wipe away the excess adhesive. Then repeat the process for the other sides of the opening.

Simple Solution

A border running above a large picture window or double door entryway may look best if the pattern is centered over this focal point, so hang that section of the wall's border first.

Restoring Damaged Wallpaper

If you have leftover scraps of wallpaper, it's pretty simple to make a patch. Simply pick a scrap that matches the area and cut the patch 4 in. larger than the damaged spot. Tape the patch to the wall and cut a circle or an oval, using a sharp utility knife, a couple of inches larger than the damaged area. Don't press too hard; you want to get through both layers, but not into the wall. Remove the patch, dampen the damaged area, remove paper and old adhesive, and then attach the patch with the recommended adhesive. Wet prepasted paper, position the patch, and smooth with a damp sponge.

What's in Store

When you're done, take a good look at your walls. Don't they look fantastic! Now, look down. What about those floors? If you're thinking about changing your floors, I'm about to show you some projects that anyone could handle.

PLAY IT SAFE!

- Make sure to allow for plenty of ventilation when working with paint, mineral spirits, and other substances containing noxious fumes.

- Immediately clean up paint spills to prevent accidental slips or falls.

- Keep paint thinners and brush-cleaning chemicals in their original airtight containers and keep them out of reach of children and pets.

- Do not flush or pour paint thinners down the drain.

- Call the environmental protection office in your area and ask where to properly dispose of oil paint and other chemicals. Oil paint should never be placed in the regular trash.

- To avoid the expense of extra paint and the hassle of disposing of it, determine in advance how much paint you will need by referring to the coverage estimates on the can label.

Floor It!

4

Did you know that cavemen actually used concrete for their floors? OK, it wasn't like the concrete we know that lines our streets or forms the foundations of our homes, but it was kind of like it. Early cave dwellers would use sand for their cave floors. Some would go a step further and mix in a little red powdery clay and a few pebbles. It was a crude form of concrete.

Can you just imagine what it would take to keep your house clean if it had dirt floors? Luckily, times have changed. Today, there are so many flooring choices—from marble to slate to wood to all different kinds of manufactured products like vinyl, carpet, and linoleum. Your family's lifestyle will play a big factor in your choice of flooring.

Getting Professional Results

In this chapter, we'll show you different ways you can take your floors from blah to beautiful. Regardless of the option you choose, though, just remember that professional results start with a *smooth, clean, dry,* and *dust-free* surface! This is one place where you really can't hide your sins: they'll always come back to bite you. If there's a big lump on your old floor, for example, and you throw a new vinyl tile floor over it, the bump will not only show under the new tile but it will also eventually lead to a crack in the new tile, and you'll end up having to replace it. Your new floors can only be as good as the underlying floor (or subfloor) that supports them.

In the case of applying new covering to floors, you really shouldn't just place it over an old floor: It's much better to remove the old floor first. However, if you insist on leaving the old floor in place, you should at least install a new underlayment (masonite or ¼ in. plywood are a couple of good choices for underlayment) between the old floor and the new one. The underlayment should be nailed or screwed to the floor joists. I usually attach it using the black all-purpose drywall screws (tech screws). Make sure to patch over all screw and nail heads and fill in seams with a flexible patching compound, sand the compound smooth, and get rid of the dust.

Now, if you are removing the old flooring, assess the stability and smoothness of the existing underlayment. You may only need to eliminate movement (see directions on nailing squeaky floors in this chapter), fill in gaps, and cover screw and nail heads. Now, you're ready to install the floor of your dreams!

Hardwood Floors

If you are an avid do-it-yourselfer, I'm sure you'll be able to install a standard hardwood floor just as you see the professionals doing. But for the beginner, I recommend installing a "floating" floor. A floating floor does just that; it isn't attached to the floor or wall. All of its tongue-and-groove planks are glued together as they are installed, which means it becomes one solid sheet of floor covering when the glue dries. (It's like a room-sized area rug made out of wood, in a way.) It can be installed anywhere you would use regular hardwood floors. Its biggest advantage over standard hardwood floors: All of the boards are prefinished, making this a simple glue and position kind of job.

How to Install a Floating Hardwood Floor

WHAT YOU NEED   **Wood planks** (How many depends on the size of the floor you're covering.)
Rubber mallet
Tape measure

Foam base kit
Wood glue
Small pry bar
Saw
Kneepad/old pillow

STEP 1   Remove old flooring and get a good-condition underlayment in place.

STEP 2   Place the wood planks in the room at least 48 hours before you start installing them so that they can acclimate to the room's conditions, like humidity and temperature. Think of it as a house settling—let the planks settle and get comfortable. Also, this is a good time to remove your quarter-round (or shoe) molding (the molding where the floor meets the baseboard) and to undercut the door frames and jam to allow room for the new flooring (see illustration).

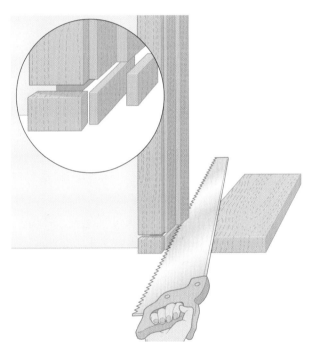

STEP 3   Lay out a foam base. It's just like a piece of thin sponge about an ⅛ in. thick and comes in rolls. Use the tape that comes in the kit to join its seams.

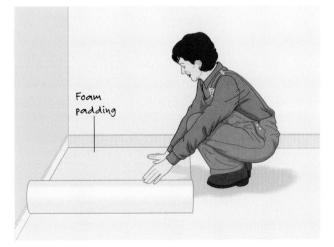

Foam padding

STEP 4 Install spacers. These are very small pieces of wood that go against the baseboard. You don't want to install your floor planks flush against the wall because then the wood will have no room to breathe. The planks will expand and contract a little bit, but if you have those spacers, you'll never notice the movement. The thickness of the spacers you'll need will depend on the kind of planks you're using. Check manufacturer's directions for size specification.

STEP 5 On either side of a plank is a tongue and groove, which makes installation so easy. Now, it's time to install the first plank. Place it in position with the groove side going up against the spacers.

STEP 6 Install planks end-to-end until one row is complete, putting glue in the grooved end. The last plank will need to be cut to length (be sure to allow room for the spacer). After the first row is complete, place the small pry bar between a spacer and the plank and just give it a little push to get all planks completely flush against each other. You want to make sure your seams are nice and tight.

Simple Solution

Always keep a moistened rag nearby. You'll want to wipe off any excess glue that gets on the floor or seeps through the seams.

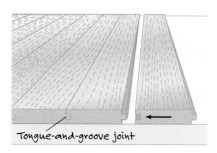

Tongue-and-groove joint

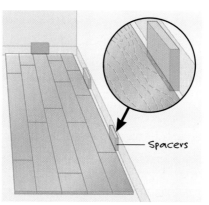

Spacers

STEP 7 Now start installing the second row of planks. Put some glue on the groove on the first plank of your second row and fit it together with the tongue of the first row. Do *not* let the seams match up. You want to offset them by about 18 in.; this will scatter the seams throughout the floor. In other words, let that first plank of the second row go past the seam in the first row or be approximately 18 in. shorter.

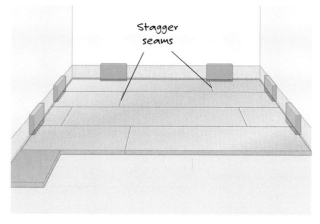

Stagger seams

STEP 8 Now you want to make sure the seam between the rows is nice and tight. Using a small piece of a plank, place the groove against the new floor plank (to keep the new plank protected), and just knock it a bit with a rubber mallet. You'll see those seams tighten up nicely.

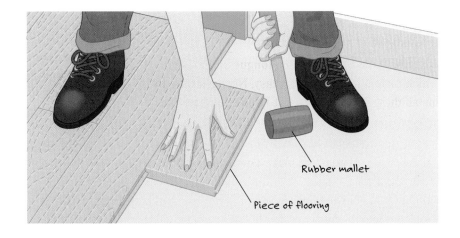

Rubber mallet

Piece of flooring

STEP 9 Proceed to install the planks until you get to the other side of the room. You'll probably have to cut planks lengthwise for the last row of flooring. Measure the remaining space on the floor and subtract ⅜ in. to allow for the spacer. That's the width to cut the plank.

STEP 10 After the glue has dried (see manufacturer's directions for time guidelines), reinstall your shoe molding. If your room didn't already have shoe molding, you'll need to buy some. As you install it, make sure that you nail it into the baseboard—not into the flooring.

Simple Solution

Go ahead and kneel on the new flooring as you install it. This will help keep the floor in place when you're knocking all those seams together. Protect your knees and flooring by kneeling on a foam pad or old pillow.

Simple Solution

You need to know what kind of finish is on your wood floor before cleaning it because cleansers are made for specific finishes. An easy way to find out is to apply a little nail polish remover on a hidden part of the floor with a cotton ball. If the remover softens the finish it is either varnish or shellac. If the finish doesn't soften, the floor is sealed with some kind of polyurethane.

Nailing Squeaky Floors

When I was growing up, my brothers and I always attempted to tiptoe around the squeaky stairs in our house trying to fool our parents about what time we got home at night. We weren't very successful. Years later, neither were my kids!

As a house settles, the layers of flooring can loosen and separate. Under the pressure of activity, these loose boards rub together, causing squeaking.

So you can see that stopping the noise is really a matter of putting the layers of the flooring back together and securing them. To do that, there are two challenges to overcome: first, figuring out exactly where the noise is coming from, and second, actually getting to the source.

Simple Solution

To temporarily stop the noise of a squeaky wood floor, sprinkle the noisy area with talcum powder. Then walk over the spot to distribute the powder. The oil from the powder will lubricate the boards to quiet them. (Wish I'd known this solution for squeaky stairs as a teenager!)

If the floor is visible from underneath (let's say it's the floor above the basement ceiling), two people working together can quickly find the troublesome spots. Someone waits in the basement or crawl space while the second person walks around on the floor above. The person below can spot where the squeak starts and mark the precise place.

Kits designed to eliminate the squeaks work by connecting the floor joist closest to the squeak to the underside of the loosened subfloor. Some feature a J-shaped hook that gets positioned around the joist and attached to an anchor bracket secured into the subfloor. Tightening the two devices together eliminates the movement and the noise!

Using a Floor Squeak Eliminator Kit

WHAT YOU NEED   **Squeak-ender kit**   **Screwdriver**
                        Drill   **Wrench**
                        Liquid thread locker   **Safety glasses**

STEP 1 Working with the joist closest to the source of the noise, insert the carriage bolt from the kit into the concave part of the anchor plate from the kit. Position this plate next to the floor joist and as close as possible to the source of the noise. Drill pilot holes and secure the plate to the subfloor with screws.

STEP 2 Slip the joist bracket from the kit around the joist and connect it to the carriage bolt. Slide on the washer and the hex nut and hand-tighten it onto the hanger bolt. Use a drop of liquid thread locker to keep the nut from working loose. As the nut is tightening, notice how the subfloor is pulled down against the joist. This tension should stop the movement and prevent squeaking in the future. Don't overtighten.

Often a drywall or plaster ceiling prevents access to the flooring from underneath and makes the squeak elimination a bit trickier. As you'll see in the next project, toenailing will help to stop movement and squeaks in this case.

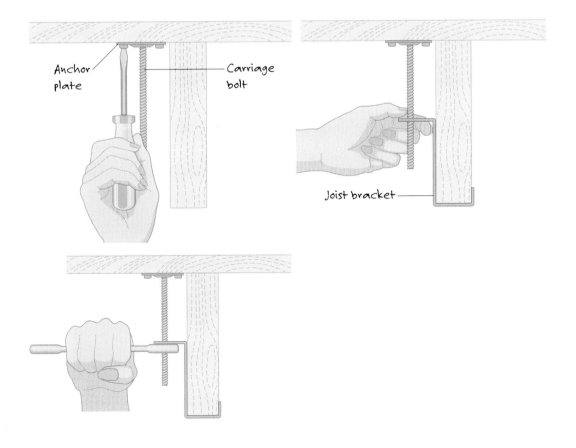

How to Toenail

WHAT YOU NEED   **Drill and Bit**   **Nail set**
                            Finishing nails   **Hammer**
                            Wood filler/stain   **Safety glasses**

Here's the approach recommended when access to the flooring from underneath is impossible.

STEP 1   In the general area of the squeak, drill pilot holes at angles using a bit just smaller in diameter than the finishing nails, so that a cross-section of the wood would show that they formed an "X." With the nails at cross angles, the layers of flooring are locked into place.

STEP 2   Using finishing nails long enough to penetrate the finished floor, the underlayment, the subfloor, and the floor joist, drive the finishing nails into the pilot holes.

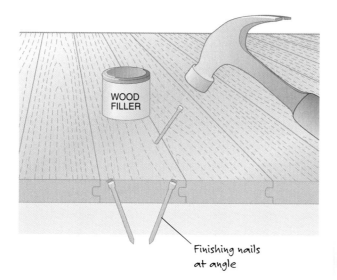

WOOD FILLER

Finishing nails
at angle

STEP 3   Countersink the finishing nails using a nail set. Get the hang of using a nail set to countersink nails on all of your projects. It will help give a professional look to your carpentry, and it's pretty simple to do. Just place the end of the nail set in the head of the finishing nail and tap until the head of the nail is recessed. Then fill the nail holes with wood filler stained to match the flooring.

Simple Solution

Hardwood floors that are inaccessible from below as well as above (such as carpeted floors) are the most difficult to fix of all, short of lifting the carpeting and toenailing the squeaks. Here's a temporary fix I've used with some success: take a 6-in. long two-by-four, place it over the squeaky area lengthwise, and pound it with a hammer. It's a good way to vent frustration, plus the pounding sometimes forces loosened nails back into place. Keep the board handy. This repair won't last forever!

Keeping Wood Floors Pristine

Protecting the surface of your flooring is very important. Sandy grit tracked in from outdoors causes the most damage to flooring. Sweeping and vacuuming regularly are a must to protect this important investment. Also, placing doormats inside and outside all entry doors will help to minimize the grit that gets tracked into the house. Finally, it's a great idea to place small cotton throw rugs in high-traffic areas or to consider the addition of room-sized rugs: Both choices can serve to protect your floors and to provide a warm, homey accent to your decor.

You can also work magic with natural-fiber rugs. They come in all different shapes, and they're made from many different fibers, such as maize from corn husks and sisal from rice fibers. Many homeowners have these rugs dyed to match their decor, but painting one of these rugs is a great way to add a personal touch and save money.

HANDY FAMILY ACTIVITY

When you go out and buy supplies for your natural-fiber rug project, get extra material so that your kids can make their own. Think about a sweet kids-made rug as a welcome mat or an area rug for their bedroom. A few days before the kids start painting the rug, have them sketch out their ideas on paper and encourage them to think about which design they like best for the rug. Then, on the big day, have them copy the design onto the rug with a pencil. This project will provide them with hours of fun!

How to Paint Natural Fiber Rugs

WHAT YOU NEED
Natural-fiber rug
Tracing paper
Utility knife
Sponge brush
Clear protective spray

Acrylic or latex paint
Pencil
Cotton swabs
Masking or duct tape

STEP 1   Transfer the design you want onto the rug. (You can use a stencil, but here we'll describe the steps required when you've created your own design.) First, trace your design onto tracing paper. Cut out the parts of the pattern you will want to paint onto the rug with a utility knife. Tape the pieces that form the pattern onto the rug. Using a pencil, trace the pattern pieces onto the rug and then remove the patterns and get ready to paint. If you want to create a border for your design, before you start painting, use masking tape or duct tape to block off a border around the perimeter of your rug.

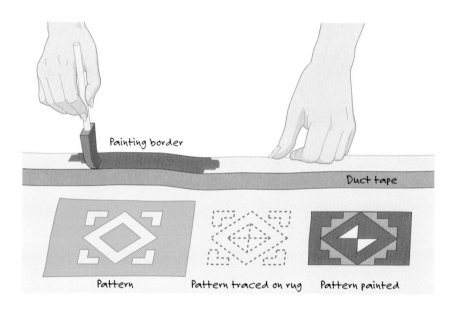

Painting border

Duct tape

Pattern   Pattern traced on rug   Pattern painted

STEP 2   You'll want to load a sponge brush with lots of paint and apply a heavy coat because the rug is going to really absorb the paint. And when you're painting, make sure that you cover all the fibers. Sometimes I use a cotton swab to push the paint in between the woven fibers.

STEP 3   Paint a border the same way using the tape to form the pattern.

STEP 4   To protect the paint after it dries (check manufacturer's directions for drying times), spray both the top and bottom of the rug with one of the clear protective coatings you can find in hardware and craft stores in the spray-paint section. This will also make it easier to wipe the rug clean as needed.

Going Vinyl

There are some rooms where you may prefer a vinyl floor. You'll usually find them in bathrooms, kitchens, laundries, and mudrooms.

How to Lay a Self-Adhesive Vinyl Tile Floor

WHAT YOU NEED

Self-adhesive tiles
Tape measure
Square
Knee pads
Tile roller or kitchen rolling pin

Pencil
Chalk line and chalk powder
Utility knife
Straightedge

STEP 1 Remove the room's shoe molding (if there is any), old flooring, and the toilet in a bathroom (see page 124 for instructions).

STEP 2 Snap chalk lines from center point to center point of opposite walls. Where the lines intersect will be the center of the room. Use a carpenter's square to make sure the two chalk lines are at 90-degree angles where they intersect. Adjust if necessary.

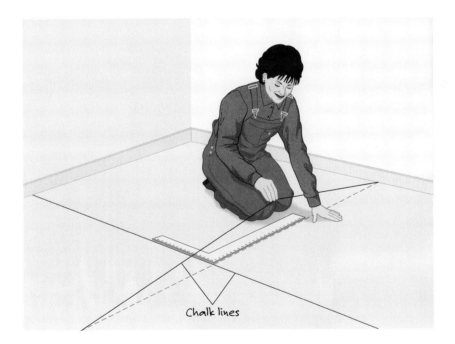

Chalk lines

STEP 3 Do a dry run along the chalk lines with tiles. You want at least a half of a tile going around the perimeter of the room. You may need to change where your chalk lines intersect to make this possible.

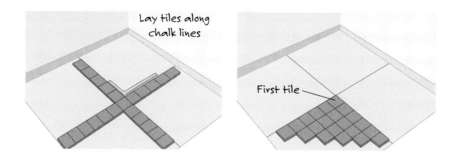

STEP 4 Now, it's time to start installing the tiles. Beginning where your chalk lines intersect, peel the backing off the first tile and carefully press it into place, making sure that it aligns with the chalk lines.

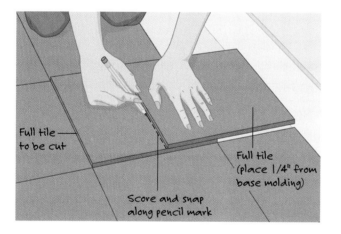

STEP 5 Continue laying the tile one quadrant at a time, in a reverse pyramid fashion, following the chalk lines and butting the tile edge to edge.

STEP 6 When you reach the perimeter of the room, you will need to cut those last tiles to make them fit. Measure the tile to be cut by placing two full tiles on top of the last full tile; then slide the top tile over so that it is about ¼ in. away from the wall. Using the top tile as a straightedge, draw a pencil line on the tile sandwiched in between.

STEP 7 Using a utility knife and a straightedge, score the tile along the pencil mark and then snap the tile in two. Peel back the adhesive and fit the trimmed tile into place. The factory-finished edge should go against the edge of the adjoining tile and the trimmed side next to the wall.

STEP 8 When all the tiles are down, roll the entire floor with a rented tile roller. Or get on your knees and use a rolling pin. (I figure that I may as well use my rolling pin for this; it's been a while since mine has been used to make pies!)

STEP 9 Install shoe molding and, in a bathroom, caulk along the tub and around the base of the reinstalled toilet.

Simple Solution

Prevent damage to your new wood or vinyl floors by placing protective pads or caps on the bottom of the legs of all your furniture.

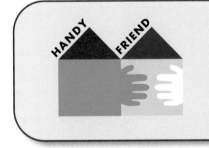

HANDY FRIEND

Pete Letteci, a professional tile installer, says, "A myth years ago was 'small room, small tile and big room, big tile.' When really you can make 13 in. tiles work in a little powder room!" He suggests letting your own eye and taste be your guide. "Do what you prefer to see every day when you walk into your home," Pete says.

How to Replace a Damaged Vinyl Tile

WHAT YOU NEED

Aluminum foil
Rags
Putty knife
Rolling pin
Plywood square

Hair dryer or iron
Adhesive remover or mineral spirits
Wax
Heavy books
Replacement tile

Place two layers of aluminum foil over the damaged tile. Soften the adhesive by applying heat with a hair dryer set on high or an iron set on medium. Move the iron across the foil or hold the hair dryer a few inches above the foil and move it back and forth.

Remove the tile and scrape away the old adhesive with a putty knife. Treat stubborn adhesive with adhesive remover or mineral spirits. Use paper towels, newspapers, or rags to blot up the adhesive. (Be sure to have good ventilation.)

Allow the area to dry before putting in your new tile. Remove the backing of a self-adhesive tile and press it into place. For tiles needing adhesive, spread the recommended adhesive to the floor using a notched trowel. Press the tile into place and wipe away any excess adhesive.

Place craft, freezer, or wax paper over the new tile and move a rolling pin across the tile. To help secure the tile, put a piece of plywood slightly larger than the tile on top of it and pile several heavy books on the wood. Don't walk on the new tile for at least two days.

Installing Carpet Squares

Carpet squares have come a long way in the last few years and, using the same techniques that you used to install your vinyl tiles, you can quickly create an attractive and durable covering for your floors. Today's squares no longer have that hard-to-remove foam backing. And even such hard-wearing and stylish fibers as Berber are now available in this format. Carpet squares are a great choice for recreational rooms, basements, and bedrooms.

For marking where you need to trim the squares, use masking tape instead of the pencil line you use for vinyl tiles. And, before cutting the squares with a carpet knife or a regular utility knife, place the square on a piece of plywood.

Simple Solution

When mud is tracked in on your carpet, don't try to wipe it up right away. Instead, let the mud dry, scrape it off, and vacuum up any residue.

Repairing a Damaged Carpet

Repairing a damaged carpet is much easier to do if you have some of the original carpet left over from when it was installed. If not, hopefully your carpet or a close cousin is available in stores.

● Small Area of Carpet Damage

For damage not more than roughly 2 in. in size, carefully trim the damaged fibers all the way to the backing with scissors. In others words, you're giving your carpet a bald spot. Use scissors or a utility knife to cut a patch from the scrap carpeting. Cut the patch as close as possible to the size and shape of the area being repaired. Trim as needed before installing, making sure the nap of the patch is running the same way as the nap on the carpet. Check the fit of the patch and trim if necessary before applying carpet cement to the back and putting it in place. Trim fibers off the top of the patch with scissors to make the patch the same height as the surrounding carpet.

Simple Solution

Blot liquid spills on carpets as soon as possible using a white absorbent material like a paper towel. Wipe from the outer edges of the spill to the center. Finally, sponge the area with club soda and blot until all traces of the spill are gone.

● Large Area of Carpet Damage

Use a heavy-duty utility knife to cut out a square of the carpeting around the damaged section. Cut all the way through the carpet backing, but not through the pad beneath. Use the section removed as a guide to cut a patch. Check to be sure that the naps on both the carpet and the patch are running the same way before cutting.

Cut pieces of double-sided carpet tape the length of the opening plus 2 in. Place half the width of the tape under each edge of the opening; the other half will be exposed in the area to be patched. (Place tape in the same manner under all edges adjoining the area to be patched.)

Match the direction of the nap on the patch and the carpet and lay the patch into place over the exposed half of the carpet tape. Press down around all seams to secure the patch to the tape.

Carefully apply a small amount of seam cement in the seams where the patch meets the carpet. Place something heavy on top of the patch overnight. A stack of books will get the job done.

Installing a Ceramic Tile Floor

Tiles are also a great way to improve the look of a floor. Before you begin installing a ceramic tile floor, I suggest that you practice by tiling the top of a table. The more practice you have at it, the better your floor will look. So for directions on tiling a tabletop, check out "How to Tile a Countertop" in the chapter entitled "Kitchens for Cooks, Family, and Friends." After you've practiced on a tabletop, you'll be able to lay a tile floor with confidence. Just follow the same directions, but this time you'll be on your knees and you'll be covering a much larger area.

Replacing Broken Ceramic Tiles

Cracked or broken ceramic tiles are not only unsightly but can damage your floor, wall, tabletop or countertop since water can seep behind the tiles and mildew can develop.

Removing the broken tile is the hardest part because you want to make sure you don't damage any of the surrounding tiles. Use a grout rake, grout saw, or rotary tool with a cutting bit to remove the grout around the damaged tile. Break the damaged tile into smaller pieces using a cold chisel and a small sledgehammer. Crack an "X" across the surface of the tile and then break it into still-smaller pieces. (You can speed up the process by drilling little holes—use a rotary tool or a drill with a ceramic bit—to form the "X." Be careful not to drill through the surface underneath the tile, though.)

Once the tile is loose, work the chisel under it and gently tap with your hammer to pry it up. Use a wood chisel to get all the old grout and adhesive off the surface below. If you happen to gouge the surface below, you'll have to repair it with patching compound before replacing the tile.

When the area is dry, smooth, and dust-free, spread ceramic tile mastic on the back of the new tile with a notched spreader. Press the tile into place.

Once the adhesive is dry, apply grout to the joints. If you're replacing just one or two tiles, you can use your fingers (wear rubber gloves!). Let the grout set about 15 minutes, and with a clean, damp sponge wipe away any excess grout diagonally across the tiles. Let stand for at least 12 hours before buffing clean with a dry, soft cloth. Seal grout as recommended by the manufacturer.

Onward

Look down at your new floors. Now take a look at the windows above them. Wouldn't it be great to have some new window treatments to go with those new floors? If you've mastered installing a new floor, there's no reason you can't beautify your windows. From simple fabric drapes to wood-carved cornices, windows need not be bland!

PLAY IT SAFE!

- Carefully sand rough wood surfaces smooth so that you and your family won't be surprised by a nasty splinter in your toe.

- Keep kitchen floors free of grease to prevent accidental slips and falls.

- Use thresholds or other transition material to secure flooring in doorways or to transition from one type of flooring to another. This will give your floors a more professional look and it will help to prevent tripping.

- Keeping doormats outside all entry doors will curb the amount of grit tracked in, and also provide a place for family and friends to wipe off snow, ice, rain, leaves, and other slippery materials.

- Place nonslip mats under area rugs to prevent slips and falls.

Window Dressing 5

Everyone knows the saying that our eyes are the "windows to the soul." Well, in our homes, it's our windows that allow our eyes to see the world outside.

Now, you'd think that as soon as the first people on Earth built some sort of home, they'd automatically have created some windows. Well, oddly enough, they didn't. Historians say that the very first windows were actually just holes to allow smoke to escape from the home's cooking and heating fires. Eventually, someone wised up and realized that these openings also let the sunshine in.

As far back as medieval times, people started to install glass panes into their windows. However, transparent glass hadn't been invented yet, so all the windows were colored or stained glass made by skilled craftsmen. Actually, as technology advanced, windows were considered valuable possessions. In the sixteenth century, people would take their windows when they moved, and they even left them to people in their wills. And in 1696, the English government had the nerve to implement a window tax on homes with more than ten windows. Needless to say, houses remained kind of dark and dreary until 1845, when the tax was repealed.

One-of-a-Kind Windows

We've all seen beautiful stained glass at one time or another—whether in a church or a Victorian mansion. It always creates a signature look of elegance for any building it graces. Now, there's no reason you have to be a professional glassmaker or spend a ton of money to have your own stained glass. I'm going to show you how to make the next best thing: *faux* stained glass. Stained glass is always a nice way not only to decorate a room, but also to provide some privacy. You could use it to create room dividers, as hanging art, or to cover those glass panes next to your front door.

Simple Solution

The easiest way to clean your windows is by using a solution of one part water and three parts white vinegar. Use coffee filters or newspapers to wipe the glass because they don't leave behind the lint or streaks that rags and paper towels do.

How to Make *Faux* Stained Glass

WHAT YOU NEED   **A clear window or piece of glass**
Faux stained-glass paint (available at hardware or craft stores)
Pattern
Toothpick
(Kits are available.)

Simulated liquid leading (available at hardware or craft stores)
Scissors
Wax paper
Utility knife

STEP 1   If you cannot remove the window you are working on and, therefore, will be working on a vertical surface, you first need to make fake leading. Just take the simulated liquid leading and squeeze lines onto wax paper. Let it cure for at least eight hours, or overnight.

STEP 2   Clean the window or piece of glass so it's dust-free and dry. Attach your pattern to the exterior side of the window with masking tape. Get it nice and secure because you don't want the pattern moving around. (Place the glass on top of the pattern if working on a horizontal surface.)

Simple Solution

You can pick a pattern from stained glass pattern books found at your local craft store, or if you want to incorporate a pattern already found in the room (perhaps from the fabric on your couches), just trace the design using tracing paper and a pencil (don't use an ink pen, because you don't want the ink to seep through the paper and onto your fabric).

STEP 3 Now, start by taking those cured strips of "lead" and placing them on the outline of your pattern's design. If a lead strip is too big, just snip to size using scissors or the utility knife. (If you are working on a horizontal surface, simply squeeze the liquid leading along the pattern.)

STEP 4 For an authentic soldered look, put small drops of the lead paint wherever your lead strips meet.

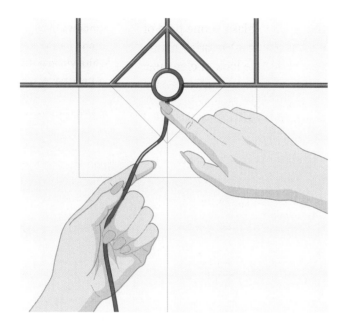

STEP 5 After outlining the entire pattern with lead, it's time to fill it in with colors. Squeezing the bottle of paint, run the nozzle along the leading and then just add a zig-zag in the middle of the glass pattern. Take a toothpick to carefully spread the paint. (Do this for each part of the pattern.) If paint gets on the leading, just wipe clean with a damp rag. If you don't like the color, just let it cure and then peel it off using a utility knife. That's the best part of *faux* stained glass: If you don't like something just peel it away.

STEP 6 Let the paint cure. Time will vary depending on how thick you applied the paint. See manufacturer's guidelines for more information.

Simple Solution

Use a small amount of mild vinegar and water solution on paper towels to clean your *faux* stained glass.

Blind-ing Light

There are several types of blinds available these days and they're made out of all different types of materials. Beyond the standard-issue horizontal ones, there are vertical and miniblind styles, and they can be found in metal, plastic, wood, or fabric. I'm not going to give you step-by-step instructions on how to install blinds, because each product is different and comes with its own special directions. However, I will give you some basic guidelines about blinds.

Most blinds' end brackets can be mounted inside the window casing, on the window frame, or on the wall. Decide how you want the blinds mounted and then measure for the width of the blind. Because anything that has to be custom-made is going to cost more, to save money, you may want to choose the installation that can use a standard size of blinds.

Also choose a blind longer than needed because it is very easy to shorten blinds, but they cannot be lengthened.

Simple Solution

Cleaning blinds can sure be a hassle, especially if you avoid doing it and allow lots of dust and dirt to build up. Get in the habit of dusting them on a regular basis with a paintbrush. Or, slip an old sock over your hand and wipe it along the blinds.

Using the right hardware and fasteners is the key to installing your blinds securely. Homes are constructed with studs at either side of the window and a header board across the top. This means that when placing the window treatments' hardware close to the window, you're likely to hit the studs. If the spot to which you want to attach the hardware does not have a stud behind it, then install wall anchors that are rated for the weight of the hardware plus the weight of the window treatment.

Blinds and curtains and our *faux* stained glass can give you both privacy and block out unwanted sunlight. Glass blocks are another great option for providing privacy and diffusing sunlight into a room. Up until recently, professionals were the only people installing glass blocks in window openings or as room dividers. But with the following system, just about anyone can install glass blocks. I must warn you, though, if you decide to build a glass wall, do not knock down a load-bearing wall and replace it with glass blocks—the blocks will *not* be able to bear the load above.

How to Install a Glass-Block Window

WHAT YOU NEED   **Glass blocks** (number of blocks depends on your project)
Silicone
Scissors or utility knife

Plastic spacers
Plastic track
Sandpaper

STEP 1   Cut a piece of plastic tracking to fit all sides of the opening being filled with glass blocks. Cut a section out of the piece that will be installed on the top of the opening, slightly larger than the width of the blocks and half the width of the tracking. This will accommodate the very last block to be installed. Don't throw the cutting away; you will reinsert it once all the blocks are in the window.

STEP 2   Install tracking on all four of the surrounding sides of your window. The piece with the cutout should be on the top. Drill pilot holes and screw the tracking in place.

STEP 3   Place the first block all the way into one of the bottom corners.

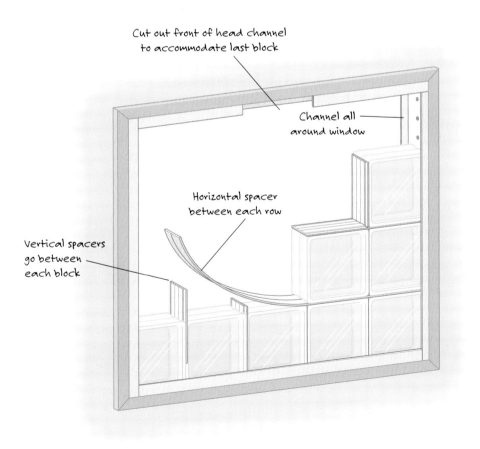

Cut out front of head channel to accommodate last block

Channel all around window

Horizontal spacer between each row

Vertical spacers go between each block

STEP 4 Place a vertical strip (plastic spacer) against that block and place the second block next to it. The channel on the vertical strip should fit snugly between the glass blocks.

STEP 5 Continue the process until your first row is complete. Before placing your second row, put a piece of the plastic spacing material across the top of the first row of blocks and then proceed to install the remaining rows just as you did the first.

STEP 6 After the last block is installed, put a small amount of silicone on the cut piece of tracking set aside earlier and then just slip it back into place between the last blocks and the window frame.

STEP 7 Now, it's time to silicone the blocks. Run your bead horizontally first and then run it vertically over all of the seams. When the two beads meet, skip over the horizontal bead and continue. Make sure to place silicone on both sides of the window.

STEP 8 Use a plastic spoon to run over the silicone and smooth it out.

STEP 9 Run a bead of white caulk all the way around the perimeter of the plastic track and the window frame inside and out to finish it off.

Now, before we get started on the next project, why not see whether your kids want to get involved in a window project of their own?

HANDY FAMILY

ACTIVITY

While you're busy creating beautiful new window treatments, your children can be busy working on colorful sun catchers. You can find kits for sun catchers at most craft stores. For older kids, you might interest them in creating a small container garden to go on the kitchen windowsill or invite them to plant their very own window box. In both cases, there are wonderful books in the library that provide kids with guidance on creating their own gardens. And in the process of helping to beautify your home, they'll also learn some important science lessons firsthand.

Fabric Treatments

Window treatments are a great way to save a lot of heating and cooling energy—even if your intent is mainly decorative. In the wintertime, during the day open up your shades, blinds, or draperies to let the sun come in and help warm up your home, and then close them at night to keep in as much of that heat as possible. But in the summertime, there are times when you'll want to close them to keep excessive heat out.

A simple fabric window treatment that's easy to make, even if you don't sew, is a roman shade. To open it, you just pull on the strings. It adds a great touch to any room.

How to Make a Roman Shade

WHAT YOU NEED
Fabric	L-brackets
Fusible tape or sewing machine	Masking tape
Iron	Cord keeper
Ring tapes	String
Hanging board	Eye hooks
Staple gun	

STEP 1 Decide if you want the shade mounted outside the window frame or if you want it to fit inside the window frame. Measure the space you want to cover with the shade. For your fabric, add about 3 in. to each side, $1\frac{1}{2}$ in. to the top and then another 6 in. to the bottom for a good substantial hem because you want to have some weight there.

STEP 2 You can sew the seams or use fusible tape. To save time, fusible tape is the best bet. Using either a sewing machine, needle and thread, or the fusible tape, make a $\frac{1}{2}$ in. hem around the entire piece of fabric, so that there aren't any raw edges showing.

STEP 3 Turn the bottom part of the fabric up $5\frac{1}{2}$ in. and attach it to the underside of the fabric using fusible tape or a running stitch. Also turn the sides and top in 1 in. and fuse or stitch.

STEP 4 Now, attach your first strip of ring tape. If you buy a roman shade kit, the tape should be included. If not, you can buy some at your local craft or fabric store. Attach the first strip along the 6 in. hem you folded up.

STEP 5 Lay the ring tape horizontally about every 6 in.

STEP 6 Attach the hanging board (cut to the width of your hemmed fabric) either by wrapping the fabric around it and stapling it on the backside or using self-adhesive looped tape (such as Velcro™) and applying as instructed.

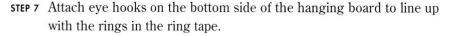

STEP 7   Attach eye hooks on the bottom side of the hanging board to line up with the rings in the ring tape.

STEP 8   Tightly tie a piece of string to the bottom ring and thread the string through all the rings in that one column all the way up to the top. Then thread through the rest of the eye hooks across the top, so all the strings end up on one side. Continue doing that with all the columns of rings until all the rings have been threaded.

STEP 9   While the shade is still slack and lying flat, gather all the strings' ends together and cut them to the same length.

STEP 10   Put the strings through a cord keeper and tie a knot to keep them in place. (To easily pull the strings through the cord keeper, hold them together with a piece of masking tape and then push the taped end through the keeper.)

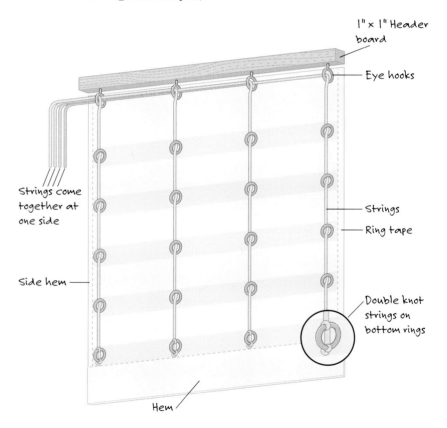

STEP 11   Now, it's time to attach the shade to the window. Just install an L-bracket on each side of the window frame. Lay the hanging board on the brackets and simply secure it to the brackets with screws.

Formal Fabric Treatment

Roman shades can be a terrific accent for just about any room in your house. For a more formal room or a traditional look in any room, you might want to consider adding cornices. Cornices give you a chance to flex your handy muscles in the areas of carpentry and upholstery; they can be made very simply by cutting straight pieces of wood, applying decorative molding, stain, or paint, or even just covering them with wallpaper. Or you can go to the other extreme and use your jigsaw to create elaborate cornices with fancy scrollwork.

In this chapter, we're going to go for a happy medium. We'll show you how to make beautiful cornices using the same techniques that you would use to recover dining room chairs (see page 159). In fact, the same techniques for recovering chair seats are used for upholstering any rectangular surface such as benches, hassocks, and even headboards.

Simple Solution

Want some privacy in a snap? There are sprays at your hardware and craft stores that can make your glass windows look as if they're etched. If you want to change the look, you can simply remove the spray with paint remover. If you want a permanent look of etched glass, etching cream is also available. Use either the spray or cream with stencils on glass or mirrors to add a decorative design.

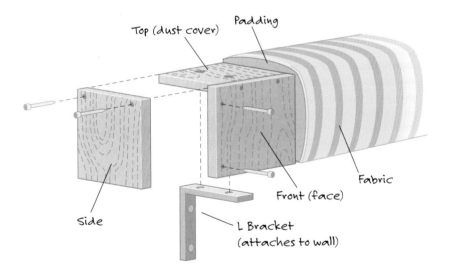

Top (dust cover) Padding

Fabric

Front (face)

Side

L Bracket
(attaches to wall)

A cornice is made of four pieces: the top (dust cover), the front, and two sides. The top should be long enough and deep enough to allow for any other window treatment to hang and operate within the confines of the cornice.

The length of the front piece is the length of the top plus the thickness of each side piece. The height of the cornice should be in proportion with the rest of the window treatment, or roughly one-eighth the length of curtains or drapes hanging on the window. Side pieces should be the same height as the height of the face and the same depth as the depth of the top.

Use these measurements to decide how much wood you will need. By adjusting the depth of the top and the length of the front an inch or two, you may be able to buy lumber in standard widths and not have to be concerned about cutting boards lengthwise.

If you're planning to cover the cornice completely with paint, fabric, or something else, lesser-grade plywood, composite board, or pine can be used. For a smoother painted finish, or a cornice that will be left natural or stained, use a finished grade of plywood or pine.

How to Make a Window Cornice

WHAT YOU NEED

1 in. pine boards or ¾ in. plywood
Wood saw—saber saw or
    circular saw
Finishing nails (1¾ in. long)
Nail set
Padding, fabric, scissors,
    staple gun (if needed)

Wood glue
Small paint brush
Drill
Drill bit
Hammer
Primer, paint, paint brush (if needed)
Safety glasses

STEP 1   Use a saber saw or circular saw to cut the four pieces of cornice according to your measurements. Allow enough from side to side and front to back for any other window treatment that you may want to install under the cornice.

STEP 2   Drill pilot holes (slightly smaller than the finishing nail) about every 3 in. and in from the edge about ⅜ in. along the sides and top of the face of the cornice and along the top of both of the sides.

STEP 3   Spread wood glue along the front edge of the side pieces and attach them to the backside of the face of the cornice. (Stand the sides of the cornice so that the edge with the glue is upright and position the face of the cornice on top of these ends. This will form an upside-down "U." Place the top piece of the cornice on its edge, under the "U" and between the sides to help support and keep the sides and face square while nailing.)

STEP 4   Apply wood glue along front and side edges of the top (dust cover) that will attach inside the front and sides of cornice. Position the dust cover and attach with finishing nails. The finishing nails will act as clamps as the wood glue cures.

Simple Solution

Using pilot holes in your wood projects will help you to keep the wood from splitting when nailing or screwing close to the ends and edges.

STEP 5   Countersink nails using a nail set. Use wood filler or spackle to fill nail holes and set the cornice aside overnight until the glue has dried.

STEP 6   Lightly sand, prime, and paint or finish the cornice as desired. If you want to cover the cornice with fabric, follow the basic directions for upholstering a chair (see page 159). One adaptation: Cut padding, available in various thicknesses at fabric stores, 2 in. wider than the cornice height and 2 in. longer than the width of the face and both sides. Use the padding as a guide to cut the fabric, adding an additional 2 in. all the way around. Staple the padding to the dust cover and underneath the sides and face pieces. Place the fabric over the padding and staple it to the underside of the cornice, beginning first at the center of the face and then at the center of the dust cover, working out to the ends. Slash the padding at the corners to allow it to be turned to the inside and staple.

STEP 7   To totally finish the cornice, staple padding and fabric over the dust cover and line the inside with fabric.

Hanging Window Treatment

Most window treatments are hung using some variation of the following technique. Just remember the three most important keys to success:

1. Install the hanging hardware into the studs or use wall anchors.
2. Use a level and double-check to be sure hardware is hanging level.
3. Hang at least one center support bracket on all window treatments wider than 40 in.

Simple Solution

Looking for an elegant window treatment? One way of achieving it is by draping or swagging fabric loosely around a rod, and just letting the fabric "puddle" on the floor, hang to the floor, or fall at any length along the sides of the window. In fact, many times you will see swagged fabric across the top of the window only, with perhaps a knotted "puff" on each end. Depending on the fabric, you may only need to hem the ends (for those who do not sew, use fusible tape) and " tuck" the salvage edges in the folds as you wrap. Whatever style you go with, in order to figure out how much fabric you'll need, drape a piece of string or rope around the rod and adjust it until you like the look. Measure the string, add at least a yard to that measurement, and that' s how much fabric you'll need for this perfect window topper.

How to Install a Window Cornice

Finished cornice   Level/straightedge
L-brackets   Stud sensor
Awl or pencil   Drill
Screws   Wall anchors (if needed)

Once your cornice is completely finished, it's ready for installation. The thickness of the material forming the top of the cornice will determine the length of screw needed to attach the bracket to the cornice.

If the bracket attaching the cornice to the wall will be placed over a stud, screws will be sufficient (make sure they are long enough to go through the thickness of the bracket, wall, and at least an inch into the stud). Anchors will be needed for installing the bracket into drywall or plaster. Single windows up to 40 in. wide will need only two brackets to hold the cornice; larger windows should have three or more, depending on the weight and length of the cornice.

Simple Solution

If you are in a hurry or maybe don't want to bring out the saw, drill, hammer, and nails, you can still make a cornice window treatment. This one isn't as sturdy and you won't be able to recover it like you can a wood cornice, but if done for a small window it will work fine. Use foam-core board. Hot glue the pieces together (face, sides, and dust cover) and then hot glue the padding and fabric to the board. To hang, attach brackets to the wall as for wood and then hot glue this lightweight cornice to the bracket.

STEP 1 Position and level the cornice and run a pencil along the underneath edge of the top of the cornice.

STEP 2 The L-brackets can be installed anywhere within several inches of the inside ends of the cornice, which in most cases will allow them to be attached into the two-by-four studs that frame the window. You can locate the studs along the pencil line using an electronic stud sensor. (If studs are not accessible, make sure to use wall anchors with your screws!) Position the first bracket so that its bend touches the pencil line and the bracket arm that is flat against the wall points down. Mark the screw holes with an awl or pencil. Drill pilot holes.

STEP 3 Install the brackets using screws long enough to penetrate the studs by at least 1 in.

STEP 4 Once the brackets are installed on the wall, rest the cornice on the brackets and push it back against the wall. From beneath the cornice top, drill pilot holes using the holes in the bracket as a guide. Be careful not to drill through the top of the cornice. Install the screws.

Nice Dye Job!

Dyeing fabric is definitely a project for everyone in the family—especially using dye found in nature. A word of warning, though: Natural dyes are not as predictable as far as the resulting color and shade (but then that's what makes it interesting).

And if you want to make window treatments—drapes, swags, sashes, and such—muslin is a great fabric to use. It's an inexpensive, 100 percent natural, woven cotton fabric that is readily available at any fabric store. What you need to buy for this project is undyed muslin, which is a natural, off-white color.

Now, deciding what to use for your dye is where the fun really begins. You can use practically anything in nature. Think of blueberries, cranberries, blackberries, tea leaves, and rose petals. Let your imagination run wild. In fact, my kids and I used to sit around and try to figure out which juices had caused an interesting stain on our clothing so that we could recreate the color. Some family favorites include:

- Tea leaves for a muted tan/beige color
- Blueberries for a bluish-pink shade
- Rose petals for a variety of hues, depending on the color of the rose used

One thing you really want to keep in mind when dyeing a lot of fabric, particularly the amount of fabric needed for window treatments, is that you'll need enough dye to do all the fabric in one shot and, if possible, a container that will hold all the fabric and dye at one time. Otherwise, if later on you decide you want more fabric dyed the same hue, you'll be out of luck because there's practically no way you can recreate a color exactly with these natural dyes.

Also, there's no way I could tell you the correct amount of water to use in proportion to the dye source because that depends on how deep you want your color to be. In other words, for deeper, darker hues, increase the amount of berries, tea leaves, flower petals, and the like in proportion to the water.

For the sake of simplicity, I use blueberries in the following steps. Again, use whatever you want!

How to Dye Muslin Naturally

WHAT YOU NEED   **Muslin** (three times the width   **Masher**
                of the window for a valance)   **Clothes dryer or iron**
                Natural dye product (see above)
                Large basin

STEP 1   Simmer the blueberries in a pot of water. Occasionally, mash the blue-berries as if you were making mashed potatoes. This helps release the blueberries' pigment. Again, the time you need to simmer the mixture depends on how many blueberries you're using in proportion to the water and how dark you want the dye. Once the water stays a consistent color and doesn't seem to be changing anymore, it's ready for dyeing.

STEP 2   While the water-blueberry mixture is still hot, pour it through a strainer into a vat large enough to hold the liquid and your fabric. Make sure that the container you're using is not made of metal and that you don't mind any permanent stains that might get on it.

STEP 3   Dampen your fabric. Ring out any excess water. Believe it or not, damp fabric will absorb the dye more completely. Add the fabric to the water-blueberry mixture and swirl it around so that the dye covers the fabric evenly.

STEP 4   After passing the fabric through the dye for about 15 minutes or so, add a bucket of ice to the liquid or transfer it to a container of ice water if you have more fabric to dye. Let the fabric sit in the cooling water. The ice-cold water helps seal in the dye.

STEP 5   When the water has completely cooled, wring out the fabric and hang it to dry *or* put it in the dryer. The heat from the dryer will set the dye and make it permanent. If a dryer is not used, heat-set the color with an iron after hanging to dry.

Obviously, window treatments are not the only thing that lend them-selves to natural dyes. And muslin isn't the only fabric you have to use. You can make tablecloths and napkins, bedding, and even clothing using this process. And there's nothing like knowing that what you're using—whether it's on your window or on your back—is 100 percent natural.

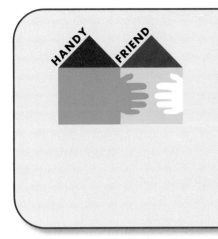

Donna Babylon, author of many books on window treatments, advises us to "Consider the window treatment as a transition between indoors and outdoors. The fabric you select should harmonize with not only the room you are decorating, but also with the view from the window." When making or purchasing window dressing: "Always line your window treatment. While you'll incur some additional costs and invest a little more time, lining extends the life of the window treatment, enhances its appearance, increases insulation, and makes light-to-medium-weight fabrics hang better."

Crash!

Sooner or later, one of your windows is going to break—whether it's just old or a baseball comes crashing in from the backyard. When buying new glass, measure from side to side and top to bottom of the space to be filled and subtract an ⅛ in. from each measurement so the piece will fit nicely on the lip of the frame.

How to Replace a Broken Window

WHAT YOU NEED   Replacement pane   Newspapers
Rubber mallet   Trash can
Hair dryer   Wood chisel
Boiled linseed oil   Sponge brush
Glazing putty   Putty knife
Safety glasses

STEP 1   To make the project easier and faster, remove the window being repaired and work on a horizontal surface. Get all of the broken glass out of the frame. Wear safety glasses and heavy-duty leather work gloves. Put something over the window like a bunch of newspapers and start tapping away with a rubber mallet. Pick out any remaining glass. Keep a trash can nearby in which to throw away the glass.

STEP 2   To remove old putty, heat it up by using a heat gun on medium or by blowing a hair dryer over it on high. Use a putty knife or wood chisel to scrape away the putty.

STEP 3   Remove glazing points. There are usually two or more on every side of the window.

STEP 4   Dip a sponge brush in boiled linseed oil and wipe it around all four sides of the frame. The oil prevents your glazing putty from drying out.

STEP 5   Put a small rope of putty on the lip (referred to as back-bed putty). This helps keep the glass from rattling.

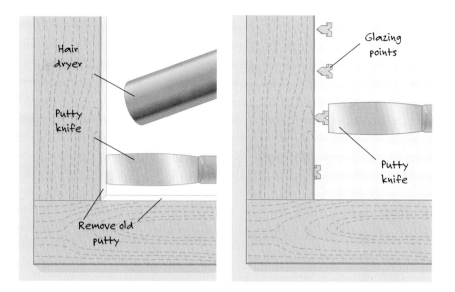

STEP 6   Position your new glass in the frame. Gently push into the back-bed putty. Reposition your glazing points using a putty knife. Place a little bit of putty around all sides of the glass. Smooth it out with your putty knife. Scrape away excess putty.

Screen Savers

I can remember going into my daughter Angel's bedroom when she was about eight years old and noticing that her window screens appeared to have the measles. She explained that she'd heard me urging my radio audience to use the nail-polish method to repair tiny holes in screens.

Since Angel was worried about bugs getting into her room through the few tiny holes in the screens, she decided to try to plug the holes with nail polish. But she missed the part where I said "Use *clear* nail polish."

Anyway, there are two basic types of screening material: aluminum and fiberglass. Aluminum is stronger and slightly more expensive than fiberglass. However, fiberglass resists corrosion and it's more flexible, so it is less likely than aluminum to tear on impact. Either type of screening is held in place in the frame the same way. A thin rubber rope called a spline sandwiches the screening material into a channel of the metal frame.

REPAIRING SMALL HOLES   Repair tiny holes with clear nail polish and small tears with a silicone adhesive. The spots may show a little, but they do keep the flies and mosquitoes from coming in for a visit.

REPAIRING LARGE HOLES You'll have to patch larger holes. You can purchase both aluminum and fiberglass screening at the hardware store. Some people save the material removed when replacing screens to use for patches, later.

Patching Fiberglass Screens

Trim off the loose edges of the hole and cut a patch of fiberglass screening about ½ in. larger than the damaged area in all directions. Spray adhesive on the back of the patch and about ½ in. all the way around the edges of the damaged area. Wait the time recommended on the adhesive can for it to become tacky, then press the patch in place.

Patching Aluminum Screens

Use utility scissors to trim off the loose edges, square up the damaged area, and cut an aluminum patch 1 in. larger than the hole, all the way around. If you are using a patch kit, the patch will be fringed. If not, remove the outer threads on your patch so that about ¼ in. of the threads from the aluminum patch are fringed, then carefully bend the fringed edges down at a 90-degree angle. Gently coax the ends through the screen over the damaged area. Jiggling the patch will help each of the aluminum threads to penetrate the holes of the screen. Fold the edges in toward the center of the patch to lock them in place.

Patch cut larger than damaged area

Replacing Screens

Over the years, screens can get pretty beat up. Sure, you can patch once or twice, but any more than that will be very unsightly. You might as well just replace the screening material. Even if there are no holes, you may want to replace the screening if it has pulled away from the frame or has been pushed out of shape.

How to Replace an Aluminum Screen in Metal Frame

WHAT YOU NEED Awl or needle-nose pliers   Flat-head screwdriver
New screening material   New spline material
Spring clamps or spring-action Splining tool
  clothespins   Sharp utility knife

STEP 1 Pry out the end of the old spline using an awl, screwdriver, or needle-nose pliers and then pull it out the rest of the way.

STEP 2 Cut new screening 2 in. larger than the screen frame all the way around. Center the screening over the frame and clamp it in place along one side with spring clamps or spring-action clothespins.

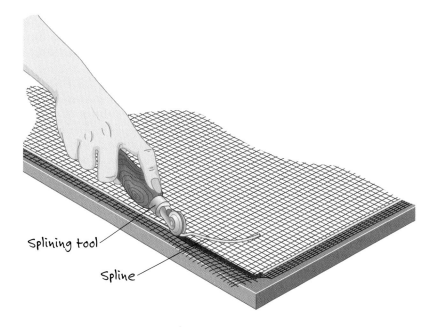

Splining tool

Spline

STEP 3 Press the screen into the channel on the frame on the side opposite the clamps using the convex side of the splining tool. Using scissors, trim across the first corner at a 45-degree angle.

STEP 4 Beginning in the trimmed corner, press the rubber spline into the channel over the screening. Use the concave wheel of the splining tool. As you get within a couple inches of the second corner, trim it at a 45-degree angle.

STEP 5 Turn the screen and move clamps so that they are always opposite the side on which you are working. Continue pressing the screen into place, followed by the spline.

STEP 6 Carefully turn the corners using a flat-head screwdriver to force the spline into the corners until all four sides are done. When you get to within a couple of inches of the last corner, cut the spline to the length needed and press in place.

STEP 7 Trim the excess screening using a very sharp utility knife, being careful not to cut the spline.

Replacing Fiberglass Screening

Installing fiberglass screening is done the same way as aluminum except that pressing the screening and spline into the channel is a one-step operation. Follow the instructions for aluminum screens, but use the concave wheel on the splining tool and roll the screening and spline into the channel at the same time.

Replacing Cracked, Crumbled, or Missing Spline

Carefully remove old splining without disturbing the screening in the channel. Press new spline into the channel using the concave wheel of the splining tool. Remove about 6 in. of the old splining at a time and immediately roll its replacement into the channel.

What's in Store

Now you have beautiful windows not only helping you to see the world outside, but also bringing light into your home. Of course, windows aren't your only source of light. That's why you should pay careful attention to the way your rooms are lit. Read on to learn about some great ways to improve not only how you see, but what you can see by creating some of your own lighting fixtures.

PLAY IT SAFE!

- When hanging your window treatment, take care not to lean your weight against the glass.

- Do not replace a load-bearing wall with a glass block wall.

- If window treatment will not be attached to a stud, then use an anchor that's strong enough to withstand the pressure and weight of the treatment.

- If you live in a high-rise building and have small children or pets, invest in some window guards to keep your loved ones safe.

- Make sure that your shade cords are secured by wrapping them around cord keepers to keep them out of reach of children (the cords could get tangled around a child's neck).

Light Up Your Life

6

It wasn't much more than 100 years ago that the electric light bulb was invented. In fact, it was early in the morning of October 21, 1879, that Thomas Edison and his staff watched their electric lamp light up with a glow that would forever change the world. Prior to Edison's groundbreaking invention, gaslights had been used for most of the 1800s to illuminate homes and businesses. Can you just imagine?!

Considering the extent to which we depend on electrical lighting to carry out all our daily activities at work and at home, I do think it's important for any do-it-yourselfer to become comfortable working around electricity. For that reason, I'm including a primer on electricity, a chapter entitled "Wired," and I'm passing along a lot of safety precautions about working with electricity throughout the book. If you proceed with caution and take the measures suggested, then you really can work on any of these lighting projects with confidence. Now, get started on the right foot by taking the time to read the next section on voltage testers and learning how to use them!

Using a Voltage Tester

On any electrical project, your first step will be to shut off the power flowing through the circuit where you are working. It's such a critical point that I suggest strongly you always use a voltage tester to guarantee that the power is off. In this section, we'll look at how to use the tester at a light switch.

WARNING   **Before using the tester, always switch off the circuit breaker or remove the fuse for the circuit you are working on.**

TO TEST A LIGHT SWITCH   Unscrew the switch plate screws and remove the plate. Holding the tester by the insulated portions of its probes, touch one probe to the metal electrical box *or* if the box is not made of metal, the ground wire (it'll be either a bare copper wire or a wire with green insulation and a green terminal screw) and touch the other end of the probe to each of the terminal screws on the switch, one at a time. While using the probe, watch the tester to see if it lights up. If the tester does illuminate, the switch is still receiving power. Go to the main power box and try again. Then retest the switch. Do not undertake any work until you've determined, without a doubt, that the power to this switch is completely off.

Simple Solution

Make sure always to turn the power off for the circuit where you will be working at the main power box. (I put masking tape over the circuit breaker I've flipped off so that no one will accidentally flip it back on.) Test the light switch with a voltage tester to be sure power is off. Don't just work on a light fixture with the light switch in the off position. You never know when someone will walk into the room and turn the switch back on.

Incidentally, several of my friends say that, to really be on the safe side, whenever they're working on an electrical project, they flip the *main* circuit breaker off and cut off *all* the electrical power to the *entire* house. That's okay, but I'd hate having to go around the house to reset all the clocks and VCRs after every project was done.

A Heavenly Circuit Breaker?

Sometimes in the hustle and bustle of everyday life, we forget that everything we say and do is absorbed by our children—especially the very young! They mimic what they see and hear, which really keeps us parents on our toes.

I'll never forget the evening that the kids and I were all gathered in the family room watching TV. Unfortunately, a huge electrical storm had hit the area, and it was playing havoc with our reception. And as the thunder became louder and more ominous, three-year-old Angel became terrified and began to cry. Her older brother Vince comforted her and tried to reassure her that all the racket was just some "angels bowling in heaven" (which is what we'd told Vince when he was young).

A few minutes later, we heard a crack of lightning and off went the electricity. As we sat in the pitch black trying to remember where we'd stashed the emergency candles, Angel piped up and asked, "Did God turn off the 'rectrizity' so he could change the light bulbs in heaven?" That really tickled all of us, but it did make me realize that she must have overheard me saying on many occasions that I had to turn off the electricity before I did this or that. It's a good lesson to learn when one is young!

All About Bulbs

Just a little about lightbulbs before we start on specific projects. The standard incandescent is probably still the most commonly used bulb, but today it's available in a startling variety. There's soft white, bright white, yellow, and pink, as well as an enormous selection of shapes and sizes. And you also have options in addition to the incandescent bulb.

HALOGEN   Presently, halogens are mainly used for task lighting, that is, as lighting under cabinets and for lamps. The bulbs are small in size and, therefore, can fit into small, unobtrusive fixtures. They are more expensive than incandescent and fluorescent bulbs, but they last longer and require about one-third less electricity than incandescent bulbs.

FLUORESCENT   The biggest advancements in lighting in the past several years have taken place with the fluorescent bulb. Compact fluorescent bulbs combine the high efficiency of the traditional, tube fluorescent, but they are sized to fit the same socket as an incandescent bulb. Meanwhile, a 23-to-28-watt fluorescent bulb has the same light output as a 100-watt incandescent, so it can save you money on your electric bill. True, the fluorescent bulb costs more; however, it will provide about 10,000 hours of service, whereas an incandescent lasts about 1,000 hours. And now that some of them can be dimmed (check the label; some fluorescent bulbs can be used with a standard wall-mount dimmer), they have come out of the garage and workshop and into the den and other living areas of our homes.

Obviously, before you choose your lighting, you have to first determine how you'll be using the room and what sorts of illumination would best support that activity. For instance, many people choose to use the bright light of a halogen for task lighting over a desk or a chair where they do paperwork or crafts. However, given the heat that halogens emit and their relatively high cost, they are generally not a popular choice for general overall room lighting.

Now, beyond thinking about the bulb used, another way to change the lighting in a room is to change what comes between the room and the lightbulb—the globe or decorative cover of a light fixture. This not only changes how much light you'll be getting and how it gets diffused throughout the area, but it can also help change the look of the room, depending on the fixture's design.

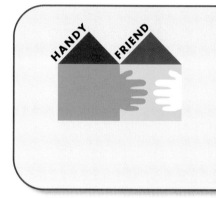

Joan Miller of Progress Lighting has lots to suggest about lighting design. For example, in the kitchen, don't feel locked into overhead lights. Think about putting lights under the cabinets, especially over countertops where you do most of your food preparation. Also, in the bathroom, don't just have lights above the mirrors that will cause shadows. Light the sides also, so the men can see to shave and women can see to apply their makeup.

Replacing a Simple Light Fixture

WHAT YOU NEED **Mounting hardware** (what you need depends on the fixture)
Screwdriver

Light fixture
Wire nuts
Voltage tester

STEP 1   Turn the power to the fixture off at the main power box and use the voltage tester on the switch (see page 92).

STEP 2   Remove the fixture's decorative cover or globe if there is one over the bulb. Remove the lightbulb.

STEP 3   Once the cover is removed you'll see the mounting screws holding the fixture to the ceiling or wall. Remove these screws. Now, you'll see the wires connecting the fixture to the wiring. (You may want a helper here to hold the fixture as you work on the wires.)

STEP 4   The wires are connected by wire nuts or screw-type terminals. Unscrew them and remove the fixture.

STEP 5 Some new fixtures can attach to your existing mounting bracket. If not, you'll need to replace the bracket. Note: Ceramic fixtures usually are screwed directly into the mounting tabs on the electrical box. Other fixtures may attach to a mounting strap or be fastened to a center-threaded stud using a connecting nut. Make sure to follow the manufacturer's directions when it comes to the mounting.

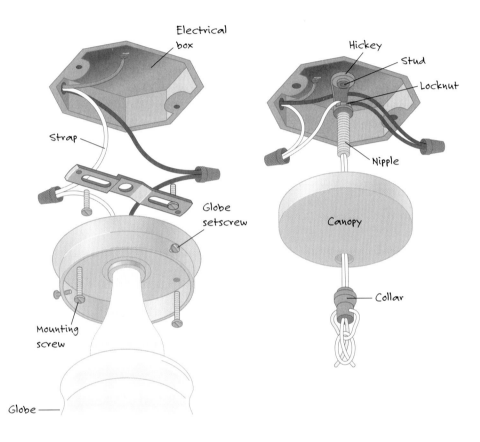

STEP 6 If your fixture requires a center-threaded stud and your electrical box doesn't have one, you can install one by first fastening a mounting strap to the box and then fastening a threaded nipple in the center hole.

STEP 7 Connect the wires (again, having someone to hold the fixture while you work on the wires is very helpful). Remember, white wire to white wire, black with black, connecting with wire nuts. Green means ground wire, and that gets attached to the green ground wire in the electrical box or the green ground screw terminal.

STEP 8 Secure the fixture mounting plate to the electrical box. Screw in the lightbulb.

STEP 9 Turn the power back on at the main box and flip the switch. I'm sure *you'll* be beaming.

Now that you've installed a new light fixture, it'll be quite easy for you to put in a new ceiling fan. But before we discuss that project further, let's see if we can get the kids involved in a fun project.

Obviously, another light source is a candle. Making homemade candles is a great activity for you and the kids. And better yet, if you use lots of candles, making your own can save you money! There are many wonderful candle-making kits; although, for younger children, the hot wax involved in making candles is too dangerous. Instead, the junior members of your clan can make candles from honeycomb sheets. You cut them to different sizes and the sheets are rolled around a wick. They smell delicious, and your children will enjoy decorating the candle base with beautiful raffia bows or small garlands of dried flowers.

A Cool Idea

Wiring a ceiling fan with a light fixture is very similar to installing any other light fixture. The biggest difference is in mounting a cross brace that will hold the weight of the fixture and withstand the motion of the fan.

If you're installing your fan in a ceiling that has access from above—an attic—it is very easy to attach a two-by-four between the joist, allowing space for the electrical box between the brace and ceiling.

In many instances, however, the fan will be installed into a ceiling that has a regular floor above it. You'll need to install an adjustable hanger through a 4½ in. hole in the ceiling where the electrical box is.

There are several types of hangers available. You should follow the manufacturer's recommendations when you buy one.

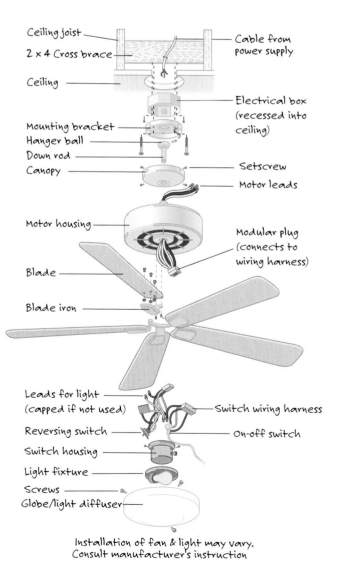

Installation of fan & light may vary.
Consult manufacturer's instruction

How to Install a Ceiling Fan and Light

WHAT YOU NEED **Mounting brace**
Mounting hardware (follow fan
manufacturer's guidelines)
Ceiling fan

Wire nuts
Screwdriver
Voltage tester
Lightbulbs

STEP 1 Turn the power off at the main power box and test the light switch with a voltage tester to make sure the circuit is *off* (see page 92). Don't work on this project with just the light switch in the off position.

STEP 2 Remove the existing light fixture. Follow the directions in Replacing a Simple Light Fixture.

STEP 3 Install the brace and electrical box, following the manufacturer's instructions. Some braces use a "U" bolt to attach to the electrical box and some electrical boxes have "J" hooks that screw into the wood cross brace.

STEP 4 Attach the mounting bracket to the electrical box. Some fan manufacturers include a special hook on the mounting bracket where you can hang the motor assembly while the electrical connections are made, so that you can hang the fan by yourself. I've installed both types of fans and, believe me, these hooks are a big help.

STEP 5 Connect the wires using wire nuts—remember white to white, black to black, and the green ground wire to green ground wire.

STEP 6 Hook the canopy to the mounting bracket, assemble the fan blades, and attach them to the motor's housing.

STEP 7 For ceiling fans with lights, remove the cap from the switch housing, then connect the electrical wiring (black to black and white to white) using wire nuts. (Note: Some manufacturers have modular plugs that make the electrical connection from the switch housing to the motor, so you don't have to do this step of connecting the wires.)

STEP 8 Secure the light kit to the switch housing by tightening the screws on the fixture.

STEP 9 Screw in the lightbulbs, restore electricity to the circuit, and give your new fan a spin.

Making a Lamp

You can make lamps out of practically anything. I've made them out of football helmets, gumball machines, birdhouses, and even a stack of books.

There are two things to keep in mind when you're picking something to turn into a lamp. First, you need to be able to drill a hole in it in order to accommodate what's called the center rod that the cord gets threaded through. Second, the lamp base must be heavy enough so that it doesn't tip over easily. But that tipping problem can usually be solved pretty quickly by adding some type of weight to the base.

The hardware you need to make your own lamp is sold in kit form at any hardware or lighting store. The rod is sold separately, though, because the length varies so much. Before you buy a rod, you want to figure out the height of the lamp base plus the height you want over and above the base to get to the bulb socket.

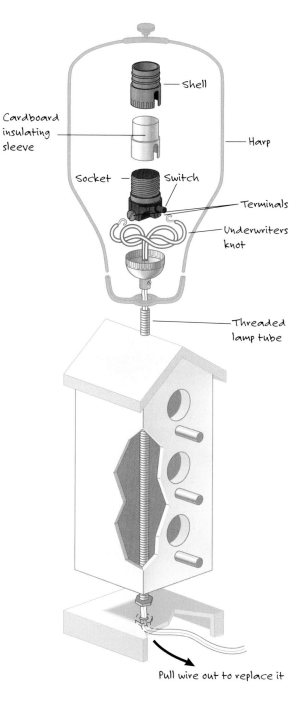

How to Make a Lamp

WHAT YOU NEED
Lamp-making kit
Lamp base
Lamp shade
Threaded rod
Wire strippers, if needed

Drill and bit large enough
    to drill a hole for the rod
Screwdriver
Safety glasses
Bulb

STEP 1   Drill a hole large enough to accommodate the diameter of the threaded rod through the object you are using for the lamp's base. (Use the right bit; in case you are drilling into ceramic, use a special ceramic bit and scratch the surface to break through the glaze at the point you need to drill.)

STEP 2   Insert the rod in the base of the lamp and secure it with a washer and nut at the bottom. Recess the nut if necessary. This can be done in some cases by drilling a hole in the bottom of the base, only as deep as the nut is thick.

STEP 3   Run the cord up through the threaded rod, slide the harp holder over the rod at the top of the lamp base, and then screw on the socket cap.

STEP 4   Split the two joined insulated wires by peeling the cord apart for about 1½ to 2 in. and tie the wires in an Underwriters knot (see page 98). Connect the wires to the terminals. The wire that has smooth-surfaced insulation gets connected to the brass screw; wrap the wire around the terminal in a clockwise direction. This is the same way you will be turning the screw to tighten it. (When tightening or loosening screws, remember: righty tightie, lefty loosie!) The wire that has the ribbed surface gets attached to the silver screw. (Most kits come with ½ in. insulation stripped from each wire; use wire strippers if necessary.)

STEP 5   Insert the cardboard insulation over the terminals, then the metal cover.

STEP 6   Attach the top of the harp and shade, screw in the bulb, place the shade on the harp, and tighten down the finial.

Dimmer Switches

One really easy way to control the amount of light in a room is with a dimmer switch.

How to Install a Dimmer Switch

WHAT YOU NEED **Dimmer Switch** (rated for the watts to fit your needs; some home chandeliers have upwards of 600 watts)
Screwdriver

Tape
Wire strippers
Wire nuts (if needed, they are generally included with the switch)
Voltage tester

STEP 1   At the main power box, turn the power off to the circuit you'll be working with.

STEP 2   Remove the switch cover. Use a voltage tester to be sure the power is off! (See page 92.)

STEP 3   Remove the two screws attaching the switch to the electrical box and gently pull the switch out of the box. Disconnect the wires from the switch by loosening the terminal screws.

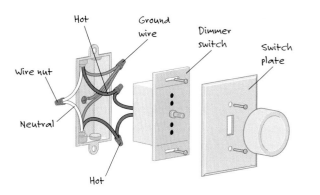

STEP 4   Connect the wires to the terminals on the new switch. The most common single-pole dimmer has lead wires coming from the body of the switch. Connect the house wires to the dimmer lead wires using wire nuts.

STEP 5   If the house wires have hook-like bends at their ends where they were previously connected to screw terminals, cut that portion off so that the wire is straight. Strip the wire a little bit more if necessary. (Should have about ½ in. of bare wire.) How to strip wires: Preset your wire strippers so that the notched opening equals the diameter of the wire. Score the insulation around the wire by closing the jaws of the strippers around the wire and open and close the strippers a couple of times as you turn the wire. Holding the strippers' jaws at the score line, close the handles and push the tool away with one hand as you hold the wire with the other.

WARNING   **Be careful to score only the insulation and not the wire. Denting, nicking, or compressing the wire can damage it and cause it to overheat and start a fire!**

If the lead wires from the dimmer consist of thin strands, gently twist the ends of each bundle of strands together.

STEP 6 After the wire nuts are secured (in this case it doesn't matter which wire connects to which), push the switch back into the box and secure it with the screws. Now, put the switch plate back on.

STEP 7 Turn the power back on and start using your new dimmer. It would be nice if, while you installed the dimmer, someone else prepared a meal. Now, enjoy a romantic dinner!

What's in Store

So now that you're thinking about electricity and lighting your home, why not take a look at one of the places where you use some of your largest amounts of wattage — the kitchen? It's here that appliances blend, chop, mix, and cook the ingredients for your meals. It's also the room where most families get to spend a lot of time together. The kitchen is not only about frozen meats and milk. It's a place where you'll sit down, relax, and talk things over with your friends and family. Why not think about making it as comfortable as possible?

PLAY IT SAFE!

- **Never undertake any electrical repairs unless you have first shut off the electricity at the main power box *or* unplugged the appliance you are working on.**

- **Use a voltage tester at the outlet or switch where you're working, to double-check that the electricity is completely turned off at the main power box.**

- **Do not use electrical appliances while standing in water.**

- **If you notice that a fuse blows or a circuit breaker trips every time you plug something in or turn on a switch on a particular circuit, the circuit is overloaded. You should unplug items not used and consider upgrading your electrical system.**

- **Kid-proof your electrical outlets with special plastic caps.**

- **If the fixture you're installing is too heavy or clumsy to handle, make sure there's someone around to help you out.**

- **If the cord to a lamp appears worn or frayed, don't use that lamp until you've replaced the cord.**

Kitchens for Cooks, Family, and Friends

7

When you hear the word "kitchen," what do you think of? Is it the mouth-watering smell of your grandmother's fresh-baked buns? Is it the breakfast time you share with your kids? How about the chocolate cake you and your best friend ate with total glee—and some guilt, of course—during a late-night chat? Or is it where mom and dad sat you down and gave you a heart-to-heart about your first love?

Kitchens really are the heart of a home. So much time is spent in the kitchen—cooking, cleaning, chatting on the phone, or just drinking coffee and reading the Sunday paper—that it becomes a place at the center of many memories.

Kitchens are also the place where children learn some of their very first lessons in life. Stoves show them how dangerous fire and gas can be. Sinks and dishwashers show them how to be helpful when they do the dishes. And of course, there's the fridge. Isn't that one of the first places they go to in the morning, after school, and for an evening snack? It's also a place where some medications are kept and even some school projects are stored (homemade dishes for the inevitable International Day at school!). And of course, kitchens are where your children will learn to cook. One day, they'll be on their own.

But did you know that kitchens weren't always such a central part of the home? Back in Colonial times, kitchens were actually detached from the home because wood-burning fireplaces were used for cooking. It was far too dangerous to have so much fire blazing in the wood-framed houses.

Food was cooked in a fireplace, either roasted on spits, boiled in kettles suspended over the fire, or heated in skillets that had little legs that elevated them above the embers of the fire. Children were often asked to help by turning the meat on the roasting spit. And would you believe that sometimes short-legged terriers helped, too? Known as turnspit dogs, they were trained to walk on a treadmill-like device attached to the spit so it would turn. Fireplace cooking lasted well into the mid-1800s, until families began to use wood- and coal-burning stoves.

As kitchens became an actual part of the homes, needless to say, they became more and more important because they not only involved food preparation but became a focal point and meeting place for families. And now that the kitchen is probably the most used room in your home, it sure can take a beating. In this chapter, I'm going to show you how easy it is to give your kitchen a facelift and to keep it looking great.

Ceramic Tile Countertops

Besides the kitchen's floor, countertops probably are used—and often abused—the most. Cutting, chopping, slicing, pounding, and the occasional burn from a hot frying pan can really destroy a countertop. Ceramic tile countertops are not only a great-looking choice, but they also can withstand a lot of use. Installing a tile countertop doesn't mean a lot of construction. In fact, you don't even have to remove your old countertop to install tiles. However, if you're going to put tiles around the sink, you'll have to remove the sink and reinstall it later.

Tiles come in many different styles and colors. Go into any tile shop, and you'll be amazed by how many choices you have. But don't get overwhelmed; have fun with it. Do you want something simple like large solid-colored blocks or something a little more snazzy, like a pastel-colored checkerboard pattern? Of course, if you're not changing anything else in the kitchen—such as the color of the walls or cabinets—you do want to make sure that the tile goes with the rest of the kitchen. If possible, bring a sample of the paint color or wallpaper on your kitchen walls. And of course, don't forget to factor in the color of your appliances.

For the sake of simplicity, I'm going to tell you how to install 4 in. × 4 in. tiles (but of course, you can use other sizes if you want). You can stick with the same color throughout or mix-and-match if you'd like. Or for much more subtle detailing, just scatter a few tiles of a different color throughout the countertop in a logical pattern (perhaps changing the color every four tiles or just having a different color in all the corners). Remember, it's your kitchen. You spend so much time there that you should truly love what it looks like. Don't worry about what other people think. They have their own kitchens!

But before we get started, I want to show you a project for children who may want to help you install your new tiles. Young children love to glue things, and that's probably why they'll offer to help you lay your tiles. Instead of telling them they can't help you, let them work on their own project. While you're installing the new tiles, children can be making decorative hotplates using small pieces of tiles on a piece of wood.

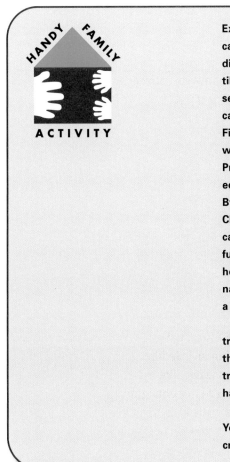

HANDY FAMILY ACTIVITY

Extra or broken tiles make great mosaic projects, or you can find small tiles (think the size of pennies, nickels, dimes, and quarters) in your local home-improvement or tile supply store. Sometimes these stores even give or sell (for a very low price) broken pieces of larger tile that can be used (just be careful of sharp and jagged edges). First, sand a piece of 12 in. × 12 in. piece of pine, plywood, or other leftover wood from another project. Prime and paint the wood a coordinating color on the edges (they will show when the project is complete). By using a thick, nontoxic glue (such as Handyman's Choice™ or Designer's Choice™), your young "helpers" can apply the small pieces of tile to the wood to create fun decorative trivets. After letting the glue dry for several hours, apply grout. Also, have your child write his or her name and the date on the back of the trivet so it becomes a precious keepsake.

This project should keep kids busy while you're concentrating on creating a beautiful new kitchen. And when they see their handiwork in the kitchen (you can hang the trivets or just lean them against a splash guard), they'll have a sense of pride that they helped, too.

Another easy project for children is making potholders. You can find inexpensive potholder kits at most toy or craft stores.

How to Install a Tile Countertop

WHAT YOU NEED **Tiles**
Coarse grit sandpaper
Spacers
Tile adhesive (depends on the kind
of tile you use—see manufacturer's
recommendations)
Notched trowel (the size depends on
the kind of tile you're using—see
manufacturer's recommendations)
Safety glasses

Tile cutter or wet saw
(can rent or buy; some
retailers lend them when
you buy the tiles)
Grout
Grout float
Soft dry cloth
Chalk line
Rags

Simple Solution

**Figuring out how many tiles you
need to buy depends on how much
surface you're recovering. Determine
the square footage by multiplying
the length by the width of the space
being covered. Then compare that
footage to the size of the tiles
you're buying and make your determination from there. Plus, I always
buy extra tiles just in case!
Mistakes do happen and, in the
future, a tile may need to be
replaced. Leftover tiles can always
be used for other projects. (Mosaics
come to mind!)**

STEP 1 Your existing countertop needs to be sanded. You
have to rough it up so the tile adhesive has something to stick to. You need only to break through the
smooth surface, so it doesn't require a lot of sanding.
After sanding, make sure to wipe off all the dust. You
may even want to use a handheld vacuum to get rid
of as much dust as possible. (If existing countertop
is in bad condition, remove it and replace with a
plywood base and cement backerboard. Attach a
1 in. × 2 in. buildup strip along the edge.)

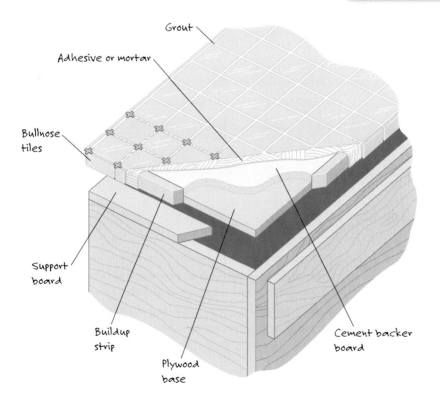

Grout

Adhesive or mortar

Bullnose
tiles

Support
board

Buildup
strip

Plywood
base

Cement backer
board

STEP 2 This is an optional step. You can install a piece of stained or painted
wood along the front edge of the countertop to finish it off *or* you can
use bullnose tiles—they have a curved, finished edge. If you will be
installing the bullnose, nail some support boards (could be one-by-twos)
to the underside of the front edge of the counter to make a temporary
lip, so the tiles on the edge don't slide off when the adhesive is still wet.

STEP 3 Don't even think of laying down any tiles until you first consider the
starting point! For an island, find the exact center of the countertop.
This is simple to do. Snap a chalk line going halfway between each side
and snap another through the middle of the other two sides. The exact
center is where these two lines intersect. (These directions are for
applying tile to an island; the starting point for a countertop attached
to the wall is normally at a corner for "L" shaped countertops or in the
center front of a straight countertop.)

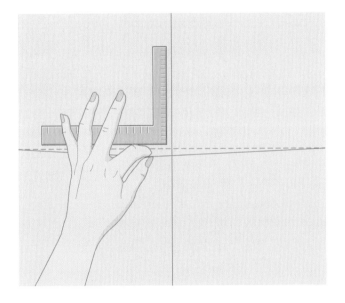

STEP 4 Put one spacer in that center or intersection and do what's called a dry
run. Basically lay the tiles down without adhesive, using spacers between
all the tiles (the spacers determine the size of your grouting). Start laying
the tiles down from the center and proceed to lay tiles to the edge. By
doing the dry run, you'll see if there's counter surface on the edge that
needs smaller-sized tiles. If so, you'll need to cut some tiles to fit the
space (for cutting instructions, see page 109). Here's a little trick to
avoid a lot of tile cutting. If possible, adjust the width of the grout lines
just enough so the tiles fit perfectly. However, make sure all the grout
lines are the same size. You really don't want different-sized grout lines;
that would look really sloppy. Adjust the tiles so that the layout is pleasing
to the eye. (Strike new chalk lines if necessary.)

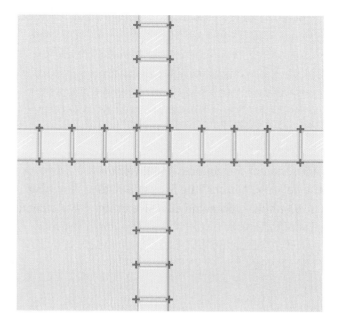

STEP 5 Remove the tiles and spacers. Now it's time to start applying the adhesive. It's very important to work in a quadrant at a time. Don't cover the entire surface with the adhesive at one time because you don't want it to start to dry before laying the tiles. Using the notched trowel (use the trowel size recommended by the manufacturer because it will leave the right amount of adhesive for your particular tile—if there's too much adhesive, it's going to squeeze out onto the top of the tiles), start spreading the adhesive on the countertop. Holding the trowel at about a 45-degree angle, smooth back and forth spreading the adhesive as close to the chalk lines, without covering them, as possible.

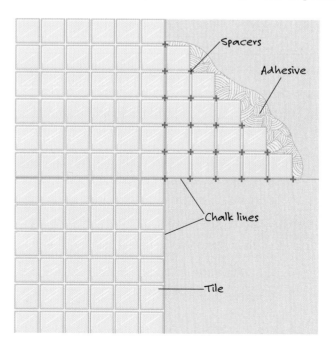

STEP 6 Lay that first spacer on top of the intersecting chalk lines. Now it's time to lay your first tile right into the adhesive in the corner of the spacer. Don't slide your tile into place because you don't want the adhesive to move. Lay the tile in position and twist it a little bit with your fingertips. Just repeat the process, following the chalk line and using spacers to make sure all the tiles are equidistant from each other. Sure, it's sort of a tedious and repetitive process, but just keep thinking of how great your countertop is going to look when you're done.

STEP 7 After covering the entire top of the counter, you'll work on its sides. Remember to use the spacers. "Butter" the backside of the tiles being used on the edges. (To butter, apply some adhesive using your notched trowel or a putty knife.) Using your spacers, continue until all the sides are covered. Again, there may be smaller pieces of tiles needed at the end, so you'll need to cut them.

CUTTING TILE You can rent or buy a tile cutter. Some tile shops will even lend you a cutter. Ask your salesperson when you buy your tiles.

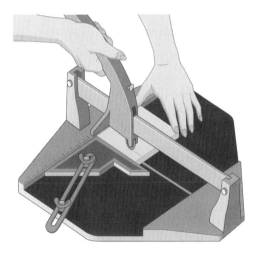

The tile cutter has a little sharp wheel that you run across your tile. This makes sort of a scratching noise. Now bring the tile back to the "snapping" area under the handle and gently push on the handle; the tile will break along the scored line. Isn't it simple to make straight cuts?

You can also use a wet saw to make straight cuts by keeping its bed completely flat.

If you need to make a miter cut, just flip one half of the bed up into a 45-degree angle and lay the tile down onto the raised half and run it across the blade.

Tiles can be scored and snapped using a handheld scoring tool, which will allow you to do not only straight cuts but also curves! If you need to make more difficult cuts, like corners, first drill a hole at the point of the corner using a special bit for ceramic and then saw along the cutting lines using a jigsaw or coping saw outfitted with special blades for ceramic.

STEP 8   After the adhesive dries (see manufacturer's recommended times and add an hour or so to be safe), it's time for grouting; filling in the space between the tiles with grout. (Remove the temporary board nailed under the front edge of the countertop if you tiled the sides.) You can get a pre-mix grout or a powder that gets mixed according to manufacturer's instructions. Grouts are available in many colors. Pour some grout on the countertop and spread it using the grout float at a 45-degree angle. Don't worry about scratching the tile with the float. It has a rubber base with a dense sponge middle so that it's soft enough to run across the tile. Now, start spreading.

Simple Solution

While buffing your new countertop, you may see some grout that still sits too high in the space between the tiles. You can remove this extra grout with a tool for striking a grout line or with a damp Popsicle stick.

Spread the grout by dragging the float diagonally across the grout lines. It's like spreading peanut butter diagonally across a slice of bread. Do this a few times over each area so extra grout is not sitting too high in between the tiles, causing "bumps" on your countertop. Also, while you're spreading the grout, make sure to remove excess grout off the tile's surface so it doesn't dry there. Just use a damp sponge to wipe it off. Continue applying the grout and wiping it down until the entire top is done.

STEP 9   As the grout dries, it's going to leave a haze on your tile. After the grout is completely dry (see manufacturer's directions on how long it should take and then add an hour or two just to be safe), take a soft dry cloth and simply buff off the haze as if you were waxing a car.

STEP 10   After several days (per manufacturer's directions), seal the grout.

After you've shined the tiles, I want you to stand back and look at your new countertop. Welcome to your new kitchen—doesn't it look great?

Keeping Tile Grout Clean

Use a mild bleach and water solution to remove most stains in the grout. Mix one tablespoon of household bleach with 4 cups of water and apply it to the stain with a sponge or spray it on and rub until the stain disappears. Rinse, buff dry, and reseal the grout.

For tougher stains, just fold a small piece of fine-grit sandpaper in half and then rub the crease along the grout until the stain vanishes. Don't forget to seal the grout to prevent future stains.

Lighten Up

Is your kitchen beginning to look a bit old and outdated? One quick and economical way to perk it up is to change the front of your cabinets. Now, this particular project calls for a cabinet door with a raised panel. If you don't have that kind of door, then you might want to consider painting the cabinets for a complete face-lift.

If your cabinets do have raised panels, the options before you are endless. All you have to do is remove that center panel and then you can replace it with a variety of materials: clear glass, etched glass, different colors of glass, or even some *faux* stained glass (see page 72).

How to Replace a Cabinet Panel with Glass

WHAT YOU NEED   **Piece of glass**   **Putty knife**
                        Glazing points   **Rubber mallet**
                        Glazing putty or caulk   **Wood chisel**
                        Safety glasses   **Work gloves**

STEP 1   Carefully take the panel out by removing the lip on the backside, by gently tapping away at it with a wood chisel and a wood or rubber mallet. Slowly remove the entire lip. (The lip is generally ¼ in. to ⅜ in. wide.)

STEP 2   Remove the panel and sand all the rough edges in the area where the panel was removed.

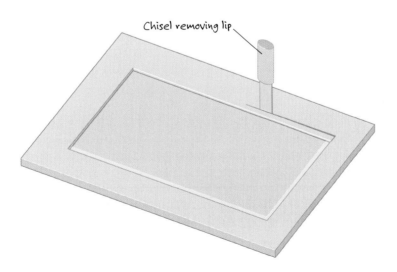

Chisel removing lip

STEP 3 Measure the panel and buy a piece of glass the same size.

STEP 4 Place the glass in the cabinet and secure with glazing points. The points can be installed with a putty knife or flat-headed screwdriver. Put points in about every 4 in. to 6 in. Be careful—you don't want to break the glass.

STEP 5 Line the seam of the glass and the wood frame with a glazing putty or caulk. This not only helps hold the glass in place, but it also keeps it from rattling. Smooth it out with a putty knife.

An Extra Compartment

Kitchens often have fake drawers in front of sinks where there isn't enough room to install a real drawer because of the sink basin. Those fake drawer fronts are basically decorative, but you can make them functional too. You can install a small tip-out tray to hold things like soap and sponges and even your rings while you're working at the sink (why risk putting rings near the sink and watching them fall down the drain?). Tip-out trays make things a bit cleaner and organized in the kitchen.

Also, if you need some space in the bathroom, tip out trays can be installed in a bathroom vanity if it has a false drawer front.

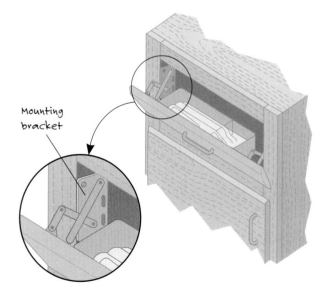

Mounting bracket

How to Install a Tip-Out Tray

WHAT YOU NEED

Pull-out tray kit
Screwdriver
Drill

Tape measure
Pencil or awl
Safety glasses

(Directions for a tip-out tray will vary from manufacturer to manufacturer; these are general instructions.)

STEP 1 Remove the false drawer front. Usually there's something called a turnbuckle on the back. Just turn it to remove the drawer front. Then remove the turnbuckles and any handles or knobs.

STEP 2 Position the hinges for the new tray on the inside edge of the cabinet frame. Make sure the bottoms are flush to the bottom of the opening and they're recessed about ⅛ in. Also, the hinges are usually marked "R" and "L" so you know which is the right one and which is the left.

STEP 3 Mark the hinge holes where the screws are to be installed and drill pilot holes. Attach hinges with screws.

STEP 4 Temporarily remove the hinges. (I know it sounds weird to install the hinges and then remove them, but believe me, I've found it is easier this way!) Lay the drawer front facedown and mark the hinge and tray location according to the tray kit's manufacturer. Drill pilot holes, but make sure not to go through to the drawer front.

STEP 5 Attach the tray to the drawer front with screws. Do not tighten the screws all the way down so the tray can easily be removed for cleaning. Next, temporarily remove the tray.

STEP 6 Attach drawer front to the hinges using the hinge holes already drilled and reinstall the hinges to the cabinet frame. Check the alignment and make sure the drawer front goes in and out easily. Replace any handles or knobs that were removed. Slip the tray in place, but don't overtighten those screws because you want to be able to easily remove the tray for cleaning.

Simple Solution

Kitchen drains can sure get a foul smell. Freshen them up and keep them free flowing by pouring ¾ cup baking soda into the drain followed by 1 cup of hot white vinegar. Let this solution sit (and yes it will bubble, but don't worry, it's a harmless "explosion") in the drain overnight and it's sure to loosen hard-water deposits and oil and grease. Just rinse away with normal use of the sink the next day. You can also make this into another project. If you have a pot that needs hard-water deposits removed, first simmer the vinegar in it. That should get rid of those nasty deposits. (Caution: this may change the chemical balance of septic tanks.)

Improving Your Swing

It's easy to take for granted little conveniences like having a refrigerator door that swings in the right direction; that is, that the door opens correctly for the work area.

Move into a new house or purchase a new refrigerator, and you might be quite dismayed to find that the door opens the wrong way. Not to worry, changing the swing of the refrigerator door is easier than you think.

If at the top of your appliance on the opposite side of the door hinges, there are holes with plastic cover plugs, you're in luck. A screwdriver, perhaps a nut driver (for screws with hex-shaped heads), and some strapping tape are all the tools you'll need to move the hinges to the other side.

Simple Solution

To keep your odd-sized baking sheets and platters organized, cut plywood to fit inside a cabinet vertically. Then drill pilot holes and install L-brackets on the plywood divider. Now position it in the cabinet, drill holes, and secure with screws.

How to Change the Door Swing on a Refrigerator

WHAT YOU NEED
Screwdriver
Nut driver (if needed)
Level

Strapping tape or masking tape
Plastic bag or bowl
Pencil or pen

STEP 1 After turning the appliance off, remove the food, shelves, and compartments on the doors of the refrigerator and freezer.

STEP 2 Use a level to see if the refrigerator is level. If not, turn the leveling feet under the front of the refrigerator until it is level.

STEP 3 Tape the freezer and refrigerator doors closed with strapping tape. To take the doors off, remove the screws that hold the hinges in place, starting at the top and working down. Remove any spacers or shims you may find under the hinges and door handles, paying attention to where each item comes from. Label them and set them aside in a safe place. Pay attention to where each screw came from as well. There can be several types and sizes of screws used, and installing the wrong screw could damage the threading. I recommend using tape to label each disassembled part and putting everything together in a plastic bag or bowl, or taping these small items right where they were removed.

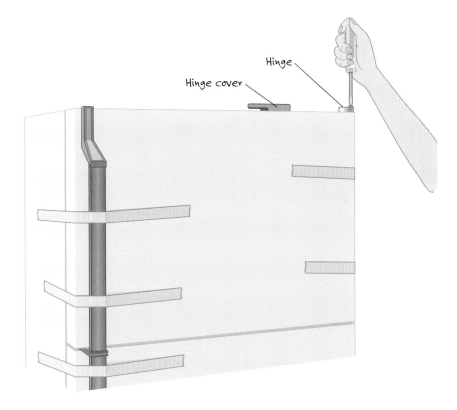

STEP 4 Once the top hinge is removed, take the tape off the freezer door, lift it off the hinge pin, and set it aside.

STEP 5 Continue removing hinges, working down from the top. Take off the tape and remove the refrigerator door as it is freed from the hinges.

STEP 6 Pry the hole cover plugs free from the unhinged side, using a plastic putty knife, and immediately install them in the opposite side where the hinges used to be. You don't want to lose those either.

STEP 7 Transfer the hinges and handles to the other side, keeping the matching parts together. Install the doors by starting at the bottom hinge and working up. When the doors are in place, check to be sure that they close snugly and that they are centered between the sides. The door seal can be adjusted by moving the top hinge and by adding or removing shims to the center and bottom hinges. Don't forget to turn the refrigerator back on when the project is complete!

Keeping It Clean

I've always tried to encourage my family to get into the habit of shucking their wet boots, coats, and umbrellas as soon as they come into the house so that we track in as little muck and mire as possible. One great way to do this is to have a convenient place to hang coats near the front door and the kitchen or back door. In many homes, you'll find a hall coat closet near the front door and a coat rack near the kitchen door.

You can create a kitchen coat rack for your family out of a length of wood and some pegs. You can fancy it up using a router to give the edges some interest. Woodworkers achieve wonderful decorative effects using this power tool. It is relatively easy to operate, with special bits that cut grooves, recesses, or shaped edges in wood. If you don't think you'll have many occasions to use one, you might want to lease one from your local hardware store or borrow one from a handy neighbor. If you do decide to use a router, spend some time working with it on scrap lumber so you have a feel for the tool. A beginning carpentry project such as making this peg coat rack is a perfect project for getting accustomed to handling the router.

Incidentally, my first coat rack ended up in the garage, but the next attempt was a success. Follow these project directions and you're sure to get it right the first time.

Doug Durbin of the nu Haus Kitchen Manufacturing Company suggests that you let form follow function when it comes to kitchen design. He says, "Sure, you may like the way a refrigerator looks in a certain spot, but make sure you don't put it in an inconvenient place that's several feet away from where you do most of your cooking."

How to Make a Coat Rack

WHAT YOU NEED

1 in. × 4 in. pine board
   cut to the length desired
Router and bit (if you want that
   fancy edge)
Ready-made wooden pegs
Drill
Drill bits

Wood glue
Rubber mallet or hammer and cloth
3 in. all-purpose screws
Wall anchors
Screw plugs
Stain, varnish, or paint
Safety glasses

STEP 1   Clamp the pine board to a work surface, or place it on top of a nonslip router pad. Insert the router bit for the edge you want, and place the router base flat against the board's surface, making sure that the edge-trimming bit you are using does not touch the edge of the wood. Turn on the power and move the router bit to the edge of the wood and gently guide it along the edge. Repeat this process for all sides.

STEP 2   Paint or stain the board and pegs before assembling, and allow them to dry. (For painting and staining, see pages 156–157.)

STEP 3   Mark on the board where you want the pegs to go, keeping in mind that they should be between 6 in. to 12 in. apart. Drill a hole for each peg, using a bit of the same diameter. Make a hole deep enough to hold the end of the peg, without going all the way through the board.

STEP 4   Apply wood glue to the end of the peg and tap it into the hole using a rubber mallet, or a hammer that's wrapped in a piece of cloth. Wipe up any excess glue immediately.

STEP 5   Attach the coat rack to wall studs using 3 in. all-purpose screws. Countersink the screw heads and cover with screw plugs, available at any hardware store; or apply wood putty, let dry, sand, and touch up with paint or stain.

What's in Store

Now that I've got you thinking about the look and function of your kitchen, I want to take you away from that room, where chaos often rules, to a place where hopefully you get some private time—the bathroom. It's a place where you're allowed to close the door to the world around you (most of the time, we hope) and spend some time on yourself. Of course, it's also the place where children learn about "bath time." I hope you'll help yourself to some quiet time in a tub full of suds and make your kids realize that "bath time" can be the best time of the day.

PLAY IT
SAFE!

- When laying tiles, or for any other project that uses strong chemicals, try to keep your windows open and a fan blowing to ventilate the room. Some adhesives and grout contain toxic fumes.

- Wear safety goggles when you are cutting tiles.

- Use heavy gloves when handling the glass fronts for your cabinets to guard against cuts.

- Get your family in the practice of immediately wiping up spills or ice from the kitchen floor.

- To prevent grease fires, don't have the heat turned too high, and never leave the kitchen with something cooking.

- Use masking tape and a pen to date and label leftovers and foods you've cooked ahead for freezing.

- Keep kitchen chemicals and cleaners out of reach of children and pets. If you must keep them in the cabinet under the sink, make sure to place a child-guard latch on the cabinet.

- Create a central message center in the kitchen so that you always know each other's whereabouts.

Bath Time!

I'd just settled in to enjoy a minute to myself one day when Christine came running up to tell me that water was all over the bathroom floor. We ran back to the bathroom to discover that the toilet was the obvious source of what was now a good-sized puddle.

The good news was that the water wasn't running out any more, so at least the situation wasn't getting any worse. Except for the fact that, now, all the kids were gathering around and I half expected to find that they'd brought friends over to watch. Sometimes I think I should have sold tickets because, during the early days when everything I accomplished was by trial and error, it really was amusing.

Anyway, Christine told me the water ran down the side of the tank each time the toilet was flushed. So I decided to take off the top of the tank, flush the toilet, and see for myself. I was looking directly down into the tank while Christine pushed the handle. A fountain of water shot straight up at my face.

I don't know how Vince got the tank top back on, or how I got under the toilet to turn off the water, but we did, laughing the whole time.

As for the repair, it was no big deal; a new gasket and cartridge in the water inlet valve solved the problem.

Meet Mr. Crapper

So who invented the modern flush toilet? Well, legend has it that a nineteenth-century English sanitary engineer named Thomas Crapper did. However, many historians say he didn't. In any case, his company did manufacture toilet tanks in England during the World War I era and inspired American soldiers stationed there to add the slang term "crapper" (and eventually "crap") to their vocabulary, which they then imported to the United States upon their return stateside.

> ## Simple Solution
>
> **Even if you never touch a plumbing project, find your home's main water supply shut-off valve and make sure it's working. In an emergency, you may need to turn off the water to your home or to an area where there's no separate shut-off valve (usually the tub and shower). The main shut-off valve is usually located near the water meter. Turn the knob to determine if it's working. If the knob is stuck, it's probably due to a buildup of hard-water deposits. Spray it with penetrating oil and try to turn the valve again.**

Crapper is not the only Englishman credited with sanitary advancements. Earlier, Sir John Harrington, godson to Queen Elizabeth I, was ridiculed when he invented a toilet back in 1596. Many devices and hundreds of years later, there were a countless number of toilet inventions. In fact, according to *Plumbing and Mechanical* magazine, the U.S. Patent Office received applications for 350 new toilet designs between 1900 and 1932.

These days, there are hundreds of styles of toilets to choose from and by law all of them are now "water saving" models. They can vary in price as much as automobiles do.

You're in the Toilet

If it hasn't already happened to you, sooner or later it will—you'll flush the toilet, only to see the water about to overflow and flood your bathroom. First of all, don't panic and flush the toilet again! That'll only make things worse. Instead, get that plunger and "plunge" right through it.

But if you're having other problems with the toilet, it usually means one of its parts is worn or broken and needs to be replaced. Following are a bunch of common problems and some really easy solutions.

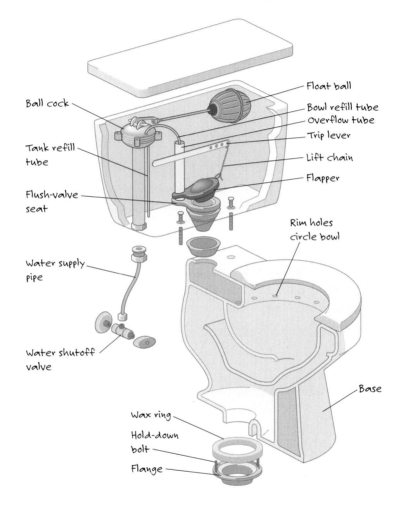

Float ball

Ball cock

Bowl refill tube

Overflow tube

Trip lever

Tank refill tube

Lift chain

Flush-valve seat

Flapper

Rim holes circle bowl

Water supply pipe

Water shutoff valve

Base

Wax ring

Hold-down bolt

Flange

HOLDING THE HANDLE   There are times when you have to hold down the handle to make the toilet flush all the way through. The most common cause for this is that the chain has too much slack and just needs to be adjusted. Move the chain higher on the hook, and your problem will most likely be solved. However, don't make the chain too taut or the flapper will not be able to close all the way and you will have constant running water in the bowl.

REPLACING A FLAPPER An easy way to tell if the flapper is causing the running water? Put food coloring in the tank. (Just a warning—it takes a lot of food coloring!) If the coloring shows up in the bowl within a few minutes, the flapper is the problem. In that case, shut off the water valve under the tank. Flush the toilet to drain the tank. Remove the flapper, disconnect the chain, and lift it from the flush handle rod. Install the new flapper and reconnect the chain, leaving it a little slack!

REPLACING A FLOAT Floats can develop tiny leaks and become waterlogged. When this happens, they don't float on top of the water. The float will never rise enough to trigger the shut-off mechanism inside the water inlet valve (also known as the ballcock valve). It's easy to replace. Just unscrew the old one and screw on the new one. Some people go for a temporary fix by bending the float rod. If you try this, *be very careful;* the rod can be hard to bend, and you run the risk of damaging the inlet valve. (When I was a kid, my dad would go into the bathroom with no tools, come out, and the toilet wouldn't run any more. I thought it was magic.)

> ## Simple Solution
>
> It's a dirty job, but someone has to do it—clean the toilet that is! For regular maintenance, just scrub the inside of the bowl with store-bought cleanser, or pour a ¼ cup of bleach in the bowl, let it set, then use a toilet brush to scrub the bowl. Sometimes, though, the rim holes in the toilet get clogged. Poke a bristle brush into the holes to de-clog them. You can even use a straightened hook on a wire hanger to get at those holes. Also, after thoroughly cleaning the toilet, put a capful of bleach into the tank about once a week to keep it glistening white.

REPLACING THE INLET VALVE CARTRIDGE (BALLCOCK VALVE) If water is dripping from the end of the tube going from the water inlet valve to the overflow pipe, and if everything checks out with the float, then you need to replace parts in the water inlet valve. Shut off the water valve under the tank. Flush the toilet to empty the tank. Take out the screws at the top of the valve and remove the top. Lift off the rubber gasket and cartridge from underneath. Reassemble using the new parts.

Have a Seat!

I must confess, for no good reason, I hate working on toilet seats and it wasn't until the one in our powder room broke right in two that I finally replaced a toilet seat that had been giving me trouble for months.

They're actually very easy to replace, and adding a new seat to your bathroom can be a quick way to give it a fresh look. I've seen some bathrooms with beautiful, traditional-looking wooden oak seats installed (one owner proudly calls his wood-seated toilet his "throne") and others with funky lucite seats with pennies embedded in them. The point is that there are lots to choose from besides just the standard-issue white. Let your own taste and vision for this room be your guide.

Now, before you decide to ditch the old one, though, make sure you know what's wrong with it. If the seat is still in pristine condition and the problem is that it's slipping around, tighten the two bolts that connect the seat to the base at the rear of the seat. Simply hold a wrench on the nut underneath and tighten each bolt with a screwdriver (sometimes the screws are hidden under a plastic cap that pops open easily).

However, a worn or cracked toilet seat will need to be replaced.

How to Change a Toilet Seat

WHAT YOU NEED   **New toilet seat**   **Locking pliers or adjustable wrench**
                     Screwdriver   **Flexible putty knife**
                     Penetrating oil (if needed)   **Hacksaw** (if needed)

The trickiest part of this job is removing the old seat without damaging the toilet. Allow enough time to do the job correctly.

If your old seat is attached with plastic bolts, just pry the plastic bolt cover up using a screwdriver or flexible putty knife. Holding the plastic nut under the seat with a covered wrench or locking pliers, unscrew the old bolts using a screwdriver.

If the seat is attached with metal bolts, it may take a little more work to get that seat off. If the bolts appear corroded and stuck in place, don't try to remove them with force or you may crack the porcelain. Instead, spray them with penetrating oil and let them sit for 15 to 20 minutes to soften the corrosion. Then loosen the bolts as directed above.

However, if oil doesn't work, remove a hacksaw blade from its frame (so that the blade will fit into the confined area you're working in) and saw the bolts free. This method is time-consuming and tedious but it will get the job done. Be careful not to scratch the toilet's finish.

Most toilet seats are of universal size; however, just to be sure you purchase the right size and shape, measure the old seat front to back, side to side and from bolt hole to bolt hole on center.

Before installing the new seat, take this opportunity to thoroughly clean the hinge area with a mild bleach and water solution, a mild abrasive cleaner like baking soda on a damp cloth, or a fine-grade scouring pad, like Scotch-brite™.

Attaching the new seat is easy. Position the seat, insert the bolts through the holes, and tighten the nuts from underneath. Be careful not to screw the bolts on too tightly or you risk cracking the porcelain and turning a simple project into a big one!

Moving Toilets Around

There are several reasons why you may want to remove and install a toilet. Perhaps your toilet is leaking around the base and you need to replace the wax ring at the bottom of the bowl. Maybe there's a crack in the bowl. Or perhaps you want to upgrade to a water-saving design or change the look of the bathroom, and your old toilet just won't do. Whatever the reason, toilets aren't difficult to remove and install. The hardest part? Dealing with the weight. Toilets are heavy and because of their shape can be quite unwieldy. In other words, you might want someone to help you when you have to lift a toilet.

Also, when you remove a toilet, it's not the prettiest of pictures. So, have some rubber gloves handy!

How to Remove a Toilet

WHAT YOU NEED **New toilet** (if you're replacing it)
Adjustable wrench
Screwdriver
Tongue-and-groove pliers or adjustable wrench
Plastic scraper
Penetrating oil (if needed to soften any corrosion)
Rotary tool with cut-off disk or hacksaw (if needed)
Old rags
Rubber gloves

STEP 1 Shut off the water supply to the toilet and then flush the toilet and hold down the handle to allow the tank to empty. Sponge out any remaining water in the tank and bowl.

STEP 2 Using an adjustable wrench, disconnect the water supply line from the shut-off valve.

STEP 3 Remove the tank. This will not only make the toilet lighter to remove, but you're less likely to crack the tank or bowl. This is important if you're only removing it and then reinstalling it because you were repairing a leak around the base or installing a new floor.

Simple Solution

Keep an old towel handy when disconnecting the water supply line from the shut-off valve. Even though the shut-off valve has been turned off, there will still be water in the line that will dribble out.

Remove the two bolts at the bottom of the tank that secure it to the bowl. Inside the tank, use a screwdriver in the head of the bolt and tongue-and-groove pliers around the nut on the outside of the tank and remove the bolts. Set the tank aside.

STEP 4 Take off the decorative plastic or ceramic caps that cover the two nuts that secure the toilet base to the floor.

STEP 5 Clean away any plumber's putty from around the nuts and base of the toilet with a plastic scraper or old credit card. Remove the nuts. If there's corrosion on and around the nuts, apply a penetrating oil to soften the corrosion. In the worst case you may need to cut the bolts. Use a rotary tool with a cut-off disk or hacksaw to do this.

STEP 6 Rock the toilet back and forth a few times to loosen and break the seal. If you're working alone, straddle the toilet and bend from your knees when lifting the base. You'll get the best grip inside, under the rim. Set the bowl aside.

STEP 7 Now it's time to put on those rubber gloves if you haven't already! To keep sewer fumes from escaping into your home, tie a long, sturdy string around a big old rag and stuff the rag into the hole in the floor. (Use the string to pull out the rag in case for whatever reason it makes its way too far into the drain and you can't reach it with your hand.)

STEP 8 Using a plastic putty knife, remove all the wax residue from around the drain opening in the floor. If you will be reinstalling the old commode, also clean the wax from the horn/flange using the plastic scraper. (The horn is the flange area on the underside of the toilet that fits in the floor drain.)

How to Install a Toilet

WHAT YOU NEED   **Toilet** (necessary hardware should   **Plumber's putty**
be included if you buy a new toilet)   **Silicone caulk**
Flexible braided steel supply line   **Screwdriver**
Adjustable wrench

STEP 1   Pack plumber's putty around the base of the new bolts to hold them in an upright position if they don't have a plastic stabilizer.

STEP 2   With the toilet bowl on its side, press the new wax ring on the horn, using just enough pressure for the ring to stick.

STEP 3   Remove the rag from the drainpipe, lift the toilet bowl, and gently lower it into position so that the bolts slide up into the base holes.

STEP 4   When the toilet bowl is in place, carefully rock it back and forth, applying downward pressure on the base at the same time to properly seal the bowl and wax ring. Sit on the toilet to seat it.

STEP 5   Install the washers and floor bolt nuts and tighten them by hand. Then, gently tighten them with an adjustable wrench, alternating from side to side, tightening the base a little at a time. Be careful; overtightening these bolts could crack the bowl!

STEP 6   Connect the supply line to the water inlet pipe under the tank. This is also a good time to replace the old supply line with a new flexible braided steel line.

STEP 7   If you removed the tank from the old toilet and are reinstalling, place new rubber washers under the tank bolt heads before securing the tank to the bowl. (For new installations, these rubber seals will be included.)

STEP 8   Connect the supply line to the shut-off valve and hand-tighten. Now, examine for leaks by turning the water on, letting the tank fill, and flushing the toilet a few times. Tighten connections if necessary.

STEP 9   If there are no leaks, run a bead of silicone caulk around the base so that water, from mopping for instance, can't seep under the toilet.

Creating a Home Spa

Looking for a way to add a little luxury to your life? Consider changing your showerhead. With a relatively small investment and a small amount of time, you can install a special handheld model with an adjustable sprayer or a deluxe model with soothing massage features. Add to it some of the wonderfully fragrant new shower gels, and your shower time can become a relaxing daily ritual.

If you've never done any plumbing projects, replacing a showerhead is a great way to get started.

How to Replace a Showerhead

WHAT YOU NEED
Showerhead
Two pairs of pliers
Thin piece of rubber
     or leather or tape

Toothbrush
White vinegar
Teflon™ tape

STEP 1 Sometimes, you can remove the old showerhead by hand. Other times, hard water deposits have built up to such a degree that it's impossible to do so without pliers. In this case, place one pair of pliers on the pipe coming from the wall and the other on the shower connector. (Protect the finish on the pipe with a piece of rubber or leather or wrap the pliers' jaws with tape.) Hold the pipe steady with one pair of pliers so it doesn't move as you loosen the head with the other.

STEP 2 If necessary, clean the threads with a toothbrush and white vinegar.

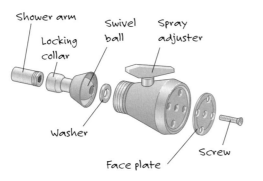

Shower arm
Locking collar
Swivel ball
Spray adjuster
Washer
Face plate
Screw

Simple Solution

The day will come when your bathtub or sink just won't drain fast enough. Chances are there's hair and yucky gunk down in the pipes. You can buy a brush at restaurant supply stores that is basically a very long, bendable rod with bristles on one end. (They are used to clean milkshake machines and coffee urns.) Just stick that brush down the drain and slowly push the rod as far as you can. Twist it a few times. More than likely, when you pull it back up, you'll be face to face with a glob of hair. If you want the kids to do this as one of their chores, warn them what they will find! When my children tried it, they were so disgusted they immediately washed the brush and the hair went right back down the drain.

STEP 3 Install the new showerhead according to the manufacturer's instructions. Some recommend that you put Teflon™ tape around the threads first. If not, there should be a rubber washer inside the connector. Most companies recommend first hand-tightening the head, checking for leaks, and then tightening it with a pair of pliers a little at a time if necessary. Be careful; don't overtighten because you can ruin the seal!

Cleaning a Showerhead

Are you thinking about investing in a new showerhead because you don't like the pressure of your current one? Well, before you go to the hardware store, try cleaning your showerhead. It could just be that stubborn debris is clogging the holes of the faceplate and diminishing the shower spray.

Heat some white vinegar to a boil and allow it to cool. Pour it into a plastic sandwich bag and submerge the showerhead into the vinegar. Use a rubber band or twist-tie to secure it to the top of the showerhead pipe. Let the showerhead soak in the vinegar for at least half an hour. If it is not fully clean, repeat, using the same vinegar.

Sometimes, you may need to disassemble the showerhead to clean really stubborn debris. First remove showerhead and soak it in hot vinegar for about a half hour. Scrub the parts with a toothbrush, and use a straight pin to dislodge any particles that are stuck in the holes of the faceplate.

It's Curtains for You

Have you shopped for shower curtains lately? Well, every so often I take a stroll along the aisles so that I can stay current in terms of the latest styles and materials. Unfortunately, I always walk away with a mild case of sticker shock. (Though nothing like the case I get when I walk into the bedding section!) Seems that the patterns and fabrics I find most appealing are also the most expensive. (What else is new? I think that happens to all of us.)

Luckily, years ago, I learned how to sew, and I enjoy it so much! In fact, I find it very relaxing and rewarding—especially seeing one of my daughters in the prom or wedding dress I've made for her! Anyway, back to the subject at hand—making shower curtains. So, when I fall in love with a store model, it's just a matter of finding fabric or a sheet that closely resembles it.

I look for sheets on sale or at discount malls—and I find that the cheaper sheets actually hang better because they have more body (stiffness). Most shower curtains measure 72 in. × 72 in. Double or full-sized sheets vary in size, however most of them are at least 80 in. × 80 in. The larger width makes for a fuller curtain, however the added length means the rod will need to be raised to accommodate it. This is easily done with a tension rod, just make sure the liner is long enough to still be inside the tub/shower. Another solution would be to hem the bottom using fusible tape or a sewing machine and keep the fuller width. In any case, it's necessary to figure out a way to hang the curtain. You can sew button holes for the hooks to go through, use a grommet kit, or sew ties to the top of the sheet or finished fabric.

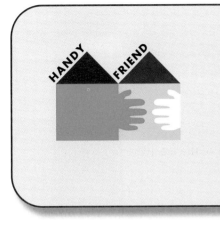

Mary Dugan, tile consultant, Ann Sacks Tile & Stone, a division of Kohler, shares recommendations for decorating the bathroom: "In bathroom design, it's a good idea to keep the permanent finishes neutral so you'll love them forever. Then you can add personality by changing the accessories seasonally, or as colors come into fashion. Your bathroom should be a reflection of your personality—remember it's the room you're in first thing in the morning and last thing at night! So you should love everything in it, especially the tile!"

How to Make a Shower Curtain

WHAT YOU NEED
Fabric *or* one full-size flat sheet
Grommet kit
Fusible web tape

Plastic shower curtain liner
Iron

To make a shower curtain from a full-size sheet, you can use the finished top edge and one finished side of the sheet, so you only need to hem one side and the bottom.

STEP 1 Cut the sheet along one side so that it measures 73 ½ in. in width (this allows for 1½ in. side hem). Cut the length of the sheet to measure 78 in.—this allows for a 6 in. hem.

STEP 2 Sew or use fusible tape to make one side seam. First: turn under ½ in. and then 1 in. to finish off the side. Press fusible tape with an iron.

STEP 3 Hem bottom by turning under 1 in. and then 5 in. This makes a substantial hem with some good weight to the curtain that will help it to hang nicely.

STEP 4 You can attach your curtain to shower curtain rings by using a grommet kit or by making buttonholes to slip the rings through. To know where to place the grommets or buttonholes, lay out the finished shower curtain and place a liner on top, positioning the liner about ½ in. from the top. Next, using a pencil, mark through the holes of the liner onto the curtain. Then make the grommets or buttonholes.

Simple Solution

Want to keep most of the water inside the tub? Here's a trick that's worked for one of my friends. Attach two medium-sized self-adhesive hooks, at shower rod height, on the walls at either side of the rod. Then take the first hole of your shower liner off the curtain ring (leave the decorative curtain on the ring) and hang it on the adhesive hook attached to the wall next to the showerhead. And once you're in the shower, hook the last hole of the liner onto the adhesive hook at the opposite end. This keeps the shower liner flush to the wall on both sides and prevents the shower from spraying onto the floor.

STEP 5 Slip the shower rings through a plastic shower liner and the fabric curtain and hang it up with the liner positioned on the inside of the tub.

Note: For a fabric curtain you will probably need to seam two pieces of material together, as most fabric does not come wide enough. Once seamed, the measurements for the unfinished curtain are 75 in. wide by 82 in. long; this allows for a 3 in. hem at top, 6 in. bottom, and 1 ½ in. for each side. Use grommets or make buttonholes as above.

Water, Water Everywhere

Drip. Drip. Drip. The sound of a leaky faucet is quite irritating. And there's no reason you should have to tolerate it.

Many years ago, when I tried to fix a dripping tub/shower faucet in the kids' bathroom, I was faced with a type I had never seen apart before: a single-handle, push-pull that turned left for hot water and right for cold. It wasn't too difficult, once I turned the water off at the main shut-off valve and got the handle off, to figure out that the cartridge needed replacing. The cartridge installed fairly easily. I fixed the leak without a hitch.

Or, so I thought. Right after I finished the job, my oldest son, Vince, hopped in the shower and let out a yell that his hot shower was ice cold. My first question was, "But, does it leak?" He replied, "No." "Well," I said, "for the time being just remember that hot means cold and cold means hot." I had installed the cartridge backwards. Oops!

Simple Solution

When taking apart a faucet—or anything, for that matter—place the parts down in the same order as you're taking them off. This makes it much easier to figure out how it all goes back together. Of course, replace any old parts with the new parts when you're doing this.

Fixing Leaky Faucets

Before starting any repair work on your faucets, shut off both the hot and cold water supply line valves under the sink (for bathtubs and showers you may have to do this at the main water valve; see page 120). Then turn the faucet on for a bit to drain any excess water in the lines.

Also, cover all drain openings. This prevents small parts from falling down the drain while you're doing your repair work. By the way, the following directions can be used no matter where the faucet is located—kitchen, mud room, etc.

How to Fix a Single-Handle Faucet (ball type)

WHAT YOU NEED   Faucet repair kit
Tongue-and-groove pliers
Rag

O-rings
Needle-nose pliers
Plumber's grease

STEP 1   Turn off hot and cold water shut-off valves under sink. Loosen set screw with tool provided in kit and remove handle.

STEP 2   Remove the cap with tongue-and-groove pliers. Use a piece of cloth between the pliers and the cap to prevent scratching.

STEP 3   Remove the ball cartridge, then carefully remove the spout. This will expose O-rings that should be replaced if water is leaking around the spout base.

STEP 4   Remove rubber faucet seats and springs using needle-nose pliers or screwdriver.

STEP 5   The repair kit will contain new rubber seals and springs. Lubricate all rubber replacement parts with plumber's grease. Replace the seats and springs.

STEP 6   Reassemble faucet, being careful to align the ball cartridge and the cam.

STEP 7   Tighten adjusting ring with repair kit tool; don't overtighten or the handle will not move smoothly.

STEP 8   After faucet is reassembled, turn on the water under the sink.

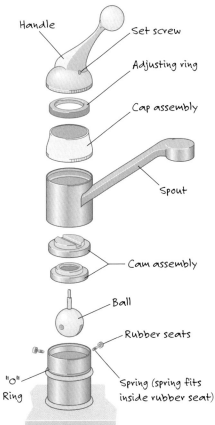

Handle
Set screw
Adjusting ring
Cap assembly
Spout
Cam assembly
Ball
Rubber seats
"O" Ring
Spring (spring fits inside rubber seat)

How to Fix a Single-Handle Faucet (cartridge, push and pull)

WHAT YOU NEED   **Putty knife**   **Needle-nose pliers**
                 Screwdriver   **O-rings _or_ cartridge**
                 Slip-joint pliers   (read directions below first)

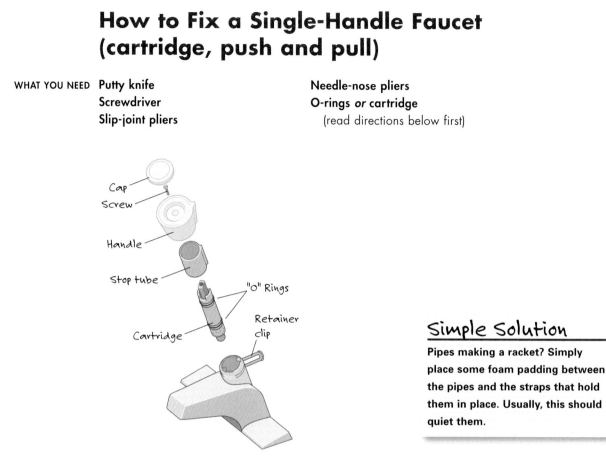

Simple Solution

Pipes making a racket? Simply place some foam padding between the pipes and the straps that hold them in place. Usually, this should quiet them.

STEP 1   Turn off hot and cold water shut-off valves under the sink. Remove handle cap, handle screw, handle, and stop tube.

STEP 2   Use needle-nose pliers to pull out the U-shaped clip that holds the cartridge in place. Pull out the cartridge, using pliers. If the cartridge appears worn, replace it. If not, just replace the O-rings.

STEP 3   If you replace the O-rings only and the faucet continues to leak, then the cartridge needs to be replaced. Insert the new cartridge with the stem pulled out from the body of the cartridge.

STEP 4   Align the "ears" on the cartridge vertically with the clip slots in valve body.

STEP 5   On most replacement cartridges, there is a red dot on one side. That side must be positioned according to manufacturer's directions; if not, you too will be getting hot water when the arrow is pointing to the cold side! Replace the retainer clip.

STEP 6   Reassemble stop tube, handle, and cover of faucet and turn the water back on.

How to Fix a Double-Handle Faucet

WHAT YOU NEED
Screwdriver
Putty knife
Rag
Rubber washer
  (read instructions below)

Adjustable wrench
Plumber's grease
Seat wrench
Seat (read instructions below)
Seat dressing tool

First, turn the water supply off for the hot and cold water. (On most doubled-handled faucets, it's necessary only to turn off the water for the handle you are working on; however, there are some that require both hot and cold be turned off, so just to be sure, turn them both off.)

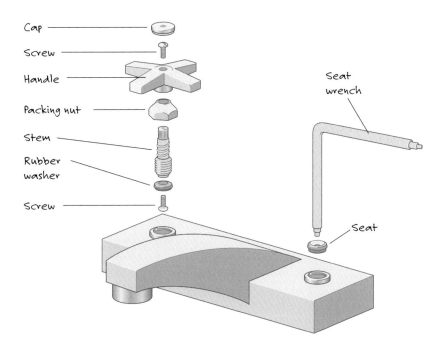

STEP 1 Loosen the screw on the top of the handle and remove the handle. If you have a "button" over that screw, you need to flip it off with a screwdriver or putty knife. Cover the tool with a piece of cloth to prevent scratching.

STEP 2 Using an adjustable wrench, loosen the packing nut and remove the stem.

STEP 3 At the bottom of the stem there is a black rubber washer held in place with a screw. Remove the screw and take the washer to the hardware store with you to make sure you get the same replacement part.

STEP 4 But before you go to the hardware store, put your finger down inside the faucet to see if the seat (the place where the rubber washer sits when the faucet is off) is rough. If the seat is rough, it should be replaced if possible. Use a seat wrench to remove and replace it. Take the old seat with you to the hardware store. If you can't remove it, you need a "seat dressing" tool to smooth its surface.

STEP 5 After the seat is taken care of, rub a little plumber's grease on the new washer, put it in place, and tighten the screw.

STEP 6 Insert the stem in the faucet and tighten the packing nut. Reassemble the faucet handle and turn the water back on.

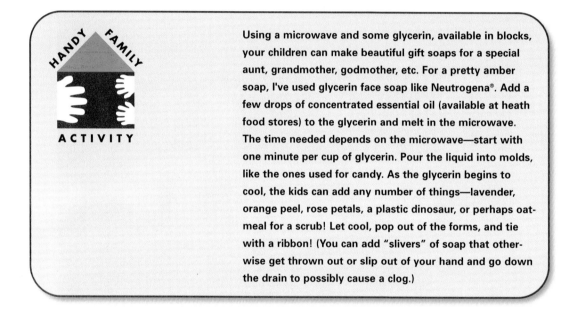

HANDY FAMILY ACTIVITY

Using a microwave and some glycerin, available in blocks, your children can make beautiful gift soaps for a special aunt, grandmother, godmother, etc. For a pretty amber soap, I've used glycerin face soap like Neutrogena®. Add a few drops of concentrated essential oil (available at heath food stores) to the glycerin and melt in the microwave. The time needed depends on the microwave—start with one minute per cup of glycerin. Pour the liquid into molds, like the ones used for candy. As the glycerin begins to cool, the kids can add any number of things—lavender, orange peel, rose petals, a plastic dinosaur, or perhaps oatmeal for a scrub! Let cool, pop out of the forms, and tie with a ribbon! (You can add "slivers" of soap that otherwise get thrown out or slip out of your hand and go down the drain to possibly cause a clog.)

How to Clean a Faucet Aerator

The short pipe screwed onto the end of the faucet spout that contains one or more screens is called an aerator. It adds air to the water so that you get a smooth stream coming out of the faucet instead of one that splashes all over the place. When the screen gets clogged, you'll notice that there seems to be less water pressure.

Follow the directions on cleaning a showerhead and let the aerator soak in the vinegar for at least an hour. If necessary, remove the aerator by unscrewing it by hand or using water pump pliers. As you take it apart, lay the parts down in the order you took them off to make reassembly easier. (Also, there should be a rubber washer inside the spout or inside the aerator. Chances are that hard water has corroded this rubber, and it's a good time to replace it if necessary. Take the washer to the hardware store with you to ensure you get the right size.) Use a toothbrush to clean the screen and a pin to remove stubborn deposits.

Installing Fresh Fixtures

At one time or another, almost every homeowner is faced with a falling towel bar or a toilet paper dispenser that needs to be replaced or reinstalled. And of course there are times when you just want to change the look of your bathroom with fresh fixtures.

Lower-priced fixtures are usually plain chrome, and you can see the screws when they're installed. Installation is really easy, but they can appear cold and industrial. Higher-priced fixtures conceal the hanging hardware for a more finished, elegant look. Since most homeowners tend to change fixtures infrequently, make sure that you can live comfortably with the way they look for a long time.

Most hanging towel bars are installed anywhere between 36 in. and 42 in. from the floor. Think carefully about where you place the bars, because if you put them on tile, you have to drill through the tile. One day, you may decide to change that bar again, and if it's in tile, that means repairing the tile, which is a lot more difficult to do than just patching up some drywall. Wherever possible, install towel bars over the studs.

Most of the towel bars I've installed came with screws and lightweight plastic anchors. I replace them with a heavier-duty anchor (molly or toggle-type anchors are the best choice). You really want the bar to hang securely, especially if you have children who think towel bars are chin-up bars!

For tissue holders, you want the toilet paper dispenser about 26 in. to 30 in. from the floor and you want at least 6 in. from the edge of the holder to the front of the toilet. Here, too, I suggest using a molly or toggle bolt for the sturdiest installation.

How to Install Towel and Toilet Tissue Hangers

WHAT YOU NEED   Tape measure   Masking tape
                Pencil   Drill
                Level   Screwdriver
                Safety glasses

STEP 1   Measure and mark the height for the bar or dispenser. Using a level, position the template (which comes with most bars) and secure it with masking tape.

STEP 2   Drill a tiny pilot hole where the template indicates screws for the mounting bracket. If the drill bit goes into a stud, it will not be necessary to use anchors. If there are no studs where the screws are to be installed, drill pilot holes for wall anchors.

STEP 3   Install the mounting brackets, insert the bar into the posts, and place the posts in position over the mounting brackets. Tighten the set screws underneath the posts.

The Mildew Mansion

Mildew is a living organism that thrives in humidity, which is why it is such a persistent problem in bathrooms. If you wash your bathroom with a solution of ¼ cup chlorine bleach to ½ gallon water, you will kill the mildew. (Wear rubber gloves, because bleach is very harsh to the skin, and have good ventilation.) Afterwards, rinse with clear water and thoroughly dry the area. Lots of cleaners will remove the stain from existing mildew but not kill the bacteria causing it. If the environment is still hospitable to mildew, it will always come back.

Left unattended, mildew is not only unsightly, but it can also damage whatever surface it is growing on. In the bathroom, that is usually the caulk and grout. Grout will weaken and crumble, allowing the mildew to get between and underneath the tiles. Even water-resistant drywall (known as greenboard or cement board) isn't absolutely resistant to the damage of mildew.

Ideally, all bathrooms should have good ventilation. This can be in the form of a window or skylight that opens, or an exhaust fan that vents outside. If you have a vent, check it regularly to be sure the pipe is clear and that birds haven't built a nest in it. If the vent goes straight up, you should be able to remove the cover and see daylight.

Make sure the fan is working by turning it on and holding a single-ply tissue close to the cover. If the fan draws the tissue in, it is working properly. Once, while taking a look at the vent in my kids' bathroom,

I found that the fan blades weren't spinning at all. Hair spray had accumulated on the rod connecting the blade to the motor and frozen it into place. (Just imagine what it was doing to our hair?!) Spraying penetrating oil around the rod solved that problem.

If you don't have enough ventilation in the bathroom, leave the door slightly ajar while bathing or showering. You can also prevent the growth of mildew around the tub/shower area by making sure that the last one to bathe wipes down the wet walls. If you run a vaporizer or humidifier in winter, cutting back on the amount of humidity can help prevent a problem. In the humid days of summer, running a dehumidifier might be in order.

What's in Store

We all know that the bathroom isn't the only place for some self-pampering and downtime. The bedroom is another. While you're thinking about your bathroom, take some time to look at your bedroom. Does it make you feel completely relaxed? Is the color scheme right for you? Do you find yourself escaping to the comfort of your room, when you just want to relax? The next chapter will show you how to transform it into the perfect oasis. And where do I think you should read this chapter? In bed, of course.

PLAY IT SAFE!

- **Always supervise your young children's bath time.**

- **A rubber mat on the bottom of your tub will help prevent slips and falls.**

- **Consider installing a grab bar on the back wall of your bath that bathers can use to steady themselves and/or to assist them in getting in and out of the tub.**

- **Make sure your family keeps the hair dryer, electric razor, curling iron, and other electric appliances away from the sink and bathtub.**

- **If you have an elderly person living in your home, make sure that the bathroom is well ventilated to prevent the possibility of heat stroke.**

- **Place child safety latches on medicine cabinets.**

Sleep Tight

9

Bedrooms have certainly changed over the years. Drafts and keeping warm were constant problems in early bedroom design. Ancient Greeks and Romans would set their beds into recessed areas in the walls to keep them away from the cold drafts. By the fifteenth century, people began decorating their beds with fancy canopies and flowing fabrics such as silk. In Italian Renaissance homes, beds were raised up on majestic platforms; and during the French empire, headboards and footboards became the norm.

These days, our bedroom design centers less around the bed and more around all of the other functions of the room. Most of you reading this book, unlike your medieval ancestors, probably use your bedroom also as a dressing room. So the efficient, organized, and attractive storage of your clothes is a prime bedroom design concern. And some of you reading this book might even use a corner of your bedroom for a home office, so accommodating that need would also drive your plans for this room.

This chapter will cover different aspects of the modern bedroom. With a nod to our ancestors, however, we'll kick it off with a look at bed ideas.

Frame It

Making your own headboard is pretty simple. You can build it from practically anything—plain wood, upholstered wood, or shutters. Some interior designers have even used outdoor fencing. As you're dreaming up ideas for your headboard, do think of all the different ways that you use your bed and make sure that it will be comfortable for all your needs. For instance, if you're someone who prizes reading a chapter of a mystery novel before slipping off to sleep, then you'll probably want to use a headboard material that you'd feel comfortable propping against as you read.

Headboards should be as wide as the bed frame plus several more inches on either side to accommodate the bedding—so that the bed when made doesn't look wider than the headboard. For example, a bed covered with a duvet will appear wider than one covered by a thin bedspread.

There's more leeway when it comes to height, although it's probably most pleasing to the eye if the height above the mattress is proportionate to the rest of the furniture in the room (or as a general rule, $1\frac{1}{2}$ ft. to 3 ft. above the pillow). Make the legs that will be attached to the frame (or wall) about 20 in. long and 10 in. wide.

Remember to stain or paint all of your pieces before you start making any cuts and attachments. You will need to use wood putty or spackling compound to fill in over nail or screw heads and then touch up with stain or paint.

How to Make a Lattice Headboard

WHAT YOU NEED **Lattice** (amount depends on the size bed)
Power saw or handsaw
Nuts and bolts
Drill and bits

Wood glue
L-braces or corner braces
Wood for two legs, top board, and mounting board
Safety glasses

STEP 1 Cut your pieces for the headboard frame to size as noted above (retaining proportions). Join the four corners the same as in making a box (see page 160) except, of course, the boards for the legs will extend beyond the lower crosspiece. Join the corners using L-braces or corner braces. Cut the lattice just larger than the size of the frame opening, making sure you leave enough on the perimeter to attach it to the framing. All gluing, nailing, and screwing happen on the back of the frame.

STEP 2 You're going to attach the two legs and the top board by placing them together to form a flush seam. First, run a bead of glue along the edge of the legs and place the leg flush with the edge of the top board. Secure each leg with an L-brace, which is placed in the middle of the joint area, by first drilling pilot holes through the brace screw holes on the backside of each corner of the joined leg and top board and then inserting the screws. Repeat this for the other leg. The brace will act as a clamp while the glue dries.

STEP 3 Attach the lattice to the frame with a bead of glue run along the frame. Position the lattice and secure it with finishing nails.

STEP 4 Attach the mounting board to the two legs with glue and L-braces. (Place the mounting board where the headboard will join the bed frame.)

STEP 5 If you want, you can add a piece of decorative molding to the top of the top board with glue and nails.

STEP 6 Position the headboard against the bed's frame and mark the holes for the bolts. Drill holes in the legs and insert the bolts through the headboard and into the frame. Apply a liquid thread locker before tightening the nuts on the bolts.

If your kids like to sew, they can make a memory blanket out of old clothes and linens. Instead of discarding their clothes, they can cut pieces off and join them with other pieces and remnant scraps. When the joined pieces are big enough to make a blanket, just sew it onto the front of a plain white washable comforter and get ready to snuggle. Every time your kids look at this blanket over the years, each scrap of fabric will bring back a flood of memories. And don't worry about making perfect seams: it's not as if you want people to think it came out of a factory.

Making Other Headboards

You can see that making the bed of your dreams is just a good idea away. Here are a few other possibilities:

- Cut a piece of one-side-finished plywood to the width of the bed frame plus 3 in. to 6 in. for each side. Cut and install moldings or apply architectural medallions and other accent pieces to dress it up.

- Round off the corners on a piece of one-side-finished plywood and paint a scene, stencil a pattern, or apply special paint techniques such as marbleizing, ragrolling, or a *faux* stone finish.

- Upholster a piece of plywood cut to size with padding fabric, following directions for upholstering a chair seat. (See page 159.)

- Build wooden cubes and arrange them around and over the head of the bed to create the look of a built-in bed, with the advantage of extra storage.

- Install a fireplace mantel over the bed.

- Shutters with fabric inserts or movable slats can be hinged together in twos, threes, even fours depending on the size of the bed.

Simple Solution

Attaching a very heavy or bulky headboard to the wall instead of to the bed frame will make moving the bed for cleaning a lot easier. Just remember to install proper anchors to the wall! To keep the bed from moving away from the wall and prevent pillows from slipping between the bed and the headboard, use carpet caster cups or rubber caster cups under the feet of the bed frame.

Pamper Your Clothes

This next home improvement is one of my favorites. It combines practical considerations with indulgence, and it's an investment that will last for years and years. Best of all, it is surprisingly easy to do.

A cedar-lined closet is one of the best improvements you can make to your bedroom. As you know, cedar is a soft, attractive, fragrant wood that contains resins that repel moths and other bugs. What better choice for a closet?

A lined closet can have cedar running either horizontally or vertically. Take into account the dimensions of the closet and the dimensions of planks or panels available when deciding how you will hang the cedar. I used 4 ft. × 4 ft. panels installed with finishing nails and construction adhesive.

Also, the planks or panels will change the dimensions of your closet so remove all hanging rods and shelves and be prepared to adjust their size before reinstalling them.

How to Line a Closet with Cedar

WHAT YOU NEED

Cedar panels or planks	Screwdriver
Pry bar	Construction adhesive
Electric stud finder	Level
Caulk gun	Finishing nails
Hammer	Flexible caulk
Nail set	Tape measure

STEP 1 Empty the closet and remove all rods and shelves. Use a small pry bar to carefully remove the baseboards and shoe molding.

STEP 2 Use a stud finder to locate the center of each stud, and mark the location on the wall.

STEP 3 You'll want to install the bottom panels first. Apply construction adhesive to the back of the cedar panel. Rest the bottom of the panel on scrap wood so that it is elevated from the floor about $1/4$ in. Nail the top corner of the panel to the wall using a 2 in. finishing nail to secure it to the stud. Do not hammer the nail in all the way.

Simple Solution

For best effect, choose a closet with doors that close snugly to keep the aroma of the cedar inside. Don't finish or seal the cedar once you're done. If the scent starts to fade over time, lightly sand with a fine sandpaper.

STEP 4 Level the panel and nail the panel's other top corner to the wall. Finish installing the first two nails and secure the panel with nails about every 6 in. along the studs.

STEP 5 Leaving a gap approximately the thickness of a penny between the panels to allow for expansion, continue to nail in the rest of the bottom panels. Make sure each panel is level and in line with the adjoining panel.

STEP 6 Install the rest of the cedar panels in the same manner.

STEP 7 Measuring from the ceiling to the last installed panel, subtract ¼ in. and cut the final panels to that measurement. Secure the panels in place, leaving the ¼ in. gap between the top panel and the ceiling. Fill this gap with flexible caulk, or install molding.

STEP 8 Remove the spacers at the floor and reattach the baseboard with finishing nails.

STEP 9 Countersink all the nail heads and fill the holes with wood putty in a color to match the cedar.

Michelle Passoff, author of *Lighten Up: Free Yourself from Clutter,* says the first step to getting things organized is to "declutter" your life. "There's a primary principle in decluttering. Get the catalogs with the catalogs, magazines with the magazines, and begin to sort your papers into categories: financial, personal, professional. You want to work your way eventually into a file system."

TONGUE-AND-GROOVE CEDAR PLANKS If the cedar planks you've purchased are the tongue-and-groove variety, install them the same way, fitting each plank into the one previously installed. Use construction adhesive on every plank and use 2 in. finishing nails where the planks cross studs as directed above.

Closet Case

Does your teenage daughter complain that she has nothing to wear? Do you find yourself stumbling over your son's sneakers? Does it take you a little too long to get ready in the morning? And is your husband starting to look rumpled? If so, HandyMa'am® says, "It's time to organize your closet space."

CLOSET CONSIDERATIONS Before you dive into a massive closet organization, it helps to take an inventory of your family's space needs. To get you started, here are some helpful rules of thumb and questions to sort out:

- Babies and children need much less hanging space and more shelf space than adults.
- Accessibility to shelves and racks is an important consideration when designing a child's closet.
- How much long hanging space is sufficient?
- Are there enough short hanging clothes to make a double-hung rod worthwhile?
- Do you need access to all your clothes, all year round?
- Is there anything that should go to charity?
- Where will you put shoes?
- Does your husband have a large tie collection? Do you have many silk scarves?
- Do your kids need special hobby shelves added to their closets?
- What gets used most often: drawer, hanging surface, or shelf space?

The answers to these questions will clarify your needs. If a standard closet kit doesn't meet your needs, then you can purchase a basic support structure that then can be customized to suit your family.

Simple Solution

Need more hanging space in a snap? If you have one rod in a closet that's high enough for two, make a lower hanging rod by attaching a length of PVC pipe to a chain and hanging it from the ends of the existing closet rod. To connect the chain to the PVC pipe, simply drill holes through either end and insert an "I" bolt through the holes; put a couple of drops of liquid thread locker on the bolt and tighten the nut. Cut each chain two times the distance from the existing rod and the place where you want the new rod to hang. Put an "S" link at one end of the chain, loop the chain over the existing rod and back to the "S" hook, and finally, attach the hook in the "I" bolt. Just make sure the top rod is anchored to sustain the added weight.

What's in a Closet Kit?

The skeleton of any closet organizing system is its basic support structure, which is installed against the back and sides of the closet walls, and the shelf brackets, which are attached to the support structure and hold the shelves, drawers, and other accessories in place.

Making sure the basic support structure is level and securely installed is crucial. Use a level when hanging the supports and install the supports in studs wherever possible. Use heavy-duty anchors for those that are not. Otherwise, sooner or later, you'll find that your closet has capsized under its own weight!

The kits usually recommend that you install closet rods at a height of 72 in. to 76 in. However, you can modify this if you want to hang double or triple levels of closet rods.

A ledger-board closet system has a permanent rail that gets attached to the wall, and then upright pieces fit over the angled ledge of the rail. Wire closet systems are snapped into plastic clips that are mounted securely on the wall. For less money but more work, you can create your own closet system using conventional shelves and supports.

Installing Closet Organizers

There are a few general rules for installing closet organizers. First, empty the closet. Carefully remove the existing rods and shelves. Patch any holes and give the closet a fresh coat of paint.

Make a level line across the back of the closet at the height you chose. This is where the support structure will be hung. If a wire closet system is being installed, the clips will be hung along this line.

Time to Get Organized

Without redoing an entire closet, the easiest and one of the least expensive ways to boost your bedroom organization is to take advantage of space that usually goes unused. Think about throwing up a series of attractive brass hooks on one wall to show off your hat collection. Or add a beautiful cedar trunk to the foot of your bed and tuck your favorite sweaters in it.

Door-mounted racks or over-the-door hanging racks are great because everything is in easy reach. Use them for storing the things you use the most, such as shoes, belts, or ties. Before actually installing, hold the organizer in place with one hand and close the door with the other. If it appears to be hitting something inside, reposition and try again. You can usually work around this problem through repositioning the organizer.

Though there is a wide variety of sizes and shapes, there are only two kinds of door storage racks—those that hang over the top of the door and those that are mounted to it. Hanging racks have hooks that fit over the top of the door. Before you purchase one, be sure to measure the thickness of your door and note if there is sufficient clearance between the top of the door and the door frame. Without it, you will not be able to close the door once the rack is in place.

Mountable racks actually attach to the door. Once again, before you install a rack, take a good look at the door to determine the tools you will need.

If the door is solid, you can attach the rack simply by screwing the brackets right onto the door. You're better off using over-the-door hanging organizers on hollow-core doors.

How to Attach Mountable Racks

First, use a level to position the rack. With a pencil or awl, mark the holes for the screws and then drill pilot holes for the screws using a drill stop or wrap tape around the bit at the point where the drill should stop so it doesn't go through to the other side of the door. Finally, secure the rack onto the door with the screws and start filling up that organizer.

Step Into My Office

If you have all your home office items tucked into one corner of your bedroom, maybe there's another place that you can hide some of these things. Do you have any empty bedroom closets or shelves or any underutilized closets elsewhere in your home? If so, one great way to help you get organized is to convert part or all of a closet into a work and office space. One of the best ways to start this is by installing cabinets in the closet. You can match them to the rest of the room, or just buy less-expensive preassembled types that can be primed and painted. Your decision will probably have a lot to do with whether or not you want to be able to close the closet doors at night and leave your "office" behind.

Simple Solution

Having trouble opening and closing your dresser drawers? Just remove the drawer, wipe any dust and dirt off tracks or wheels, apply some penetrating oil, and wipe off any excess. While you're at it, why not place some dryer sheets in the drawers? This will keep clothes fresh smelling. Replace the sheet about once a month. You can also freshen the drawers with fragrant bath soap slivers or potpourri pouches or even some of those magazine perfume strips.

Installing Cabinets in Closets

WHAT YOU NEED **Cabinets**   **Ledger board**
Drill   **Screws**
Level   **Masking tape**
Stud finder   **Safety glasses**

STEP 1 Decide where you want your cabinets to be and make a level line to locate the bottoms of the cabinets. Next, locate the studs on the wall and mark them with masking tape.

STEP 2 Install a ledger board—a regular two-by-four should work—where the bottom of the cabinets will go. Drill pilot holes in the two-by-four where it will attach to studs and install the middle screw and, before completely tightening the first screw, check to make sure it's level. Install the rest of the screws.

STEP 3 Take the door and hinges off the first cabinet and lift it onto the top of the ledger board. Install a screw through the back of the cabinet and into the center of the stud you're attaching it to. Don't tighten all the way, because you first want to make sure it's plumb and level—side to side and front to back. Now, go ahead and insert screws on the top and bottom and on the side next to the wall. (If it's not level, adjust using shims and then install screws.)

Your Private Space

Because more people are working out of their homes, either telecommuting to a distant company or running a home-based business, they're having to find ways to accommodate and balance their private and professional lives within the same space. If you do have your office space sharing personal space in your home, whether it's in a corner of the bedroom or part of the living room, you might like the idea of being able to cordon it off for part or all of the day. One great way to do this, especially if it's a temporary arrangement, is to create a room-dividing screen.

Now, there's no reason you have to make a screen totally from scratch. Bi-fold closet doors, screen doors with the screening removed and replaced with fabric, even exterior shutters can be hinged together into a folding screen. Use your imagination! And when it comes to decorating them, you can do practically anything—paint, stain, fabric covering, decoupage, you name it. Fabric is a particularly popular choice, perhaps because it can be easily changed to match the shifting decor of your house.

How to Make a Folding Screen

WHAT YOU NEED **Three or more wood panels**
Four to six butt hinges (depending on how high the screen is)

STEP 1 Once you've selected and decorated the panels, decide on the hinges. Three-way hinges designed especially for room screens bend in either direction so that the panels can be folded toward the front or back. Butt hinges can also be used and they are easier to find. Plan how you want the screen panels to fold before installing them. Long continuous piano hinges are another option.

STEP 2 Installing the hinges takes thought, time, and patience. Don't rush this step! Make sure your planned placement complements the way you'll be using the screen.

STEP 3 Join the first two panels by laying one on top of the other with right sides facing each other and the bottoms aligned. Place spacers (coins work well) the thickness of the hinge pin between the panels and clamp the panels together. After deciding where the hinges will go, hold them in place and mark the screw holes.

STEP 4 Drill pilot holes for the screws and install the hinges. On the opposite side of the middle panel, use the same method to install the hinges for the third and any subsequent panels.

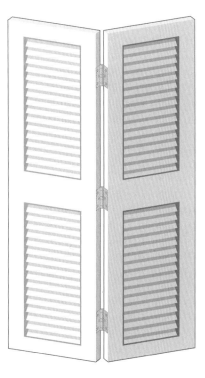

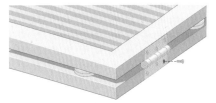

What's in Store

I hope I've inspired you to take the clutter out of your bedroom so you can flop on the bed and relax without worrying about straightening up. And when you open your eyes, I hope you see projects you've completed and, most importantly, are happy with.

There are other places, of course, where we all like to spread out and relax, especially living rooms and family dens (if you have one). Now, I'd like to show you ways to add personal accents to each room that'll add even more warmth and style. These touches include everything from simple picture frames made from leftover crown molding to restoring that beautiful antique dresser that's been in your family for generations. All are accents that say "home"!

PLAY IT SAFE!

- **Install an intercom in infants' and young children's bedrooms so that you can hear them in case of an emergency.**

- **In closets, try to make sure that heavy items are stored on low shelves to prevent the objects from falling on your family members and injuring them.**

- **Don't allow kids to use their beds as trampolines.**

- **Make sure their bedding and pajamas are made out of nonflammable material.**

- **Put your baby on his or her back in the crib.**

- **Position your children's cribs or beds far enough away from their bedroom wall so that they can't fall between the two and strangle.**

- **Encourage your kids to put away their toys at night so they can make a speedy exit in the event of an emergency.**

- **Install a smoke alarm on the ceiling just inside the door of each bedroom.**

Accents That Say Home

10

What do you picture when you think of a house being a home? Maybe it's a cozy table in a breakfast nook, where your grandparents ate breakfast together every morning of their married lives; or it's the kitchen island where you and your family gather to exchange the day's events and have a bite to eat. Or is it your child's latest works of art tacked on the refrigerator? Or maybe it's even a cushy chair that you sink into with an irresistible book or to listen to your favorite music? Whatever it is, we all treasure those special times and memories that say "home." When we see them, we know we're in our very own special place.

One of the ways that you can fill your home with special memories is to restore some of your family's heirlooms and press them into use. In this chapter, we're going to show you how to bring back the original luster of these antiques and how to finish them so they'll withstand the test of time and be around for many more generations to come. We'll also look

at things that you and your children can create that will accent
your home.

Restoring Furniture

Recently, I refinished some chairs my dad had in a barber shop he
owned when I was a kid. What memories that project brought back!
As I worked on them, I remembered all of the colorful and friendly cus-
tomers who passed through his shop. I always enjoyed my times there.
And then there's the dresser my grandmother owned that has passed
through so many different family members over the years. As soon as I
inherited it, I carefully refinished it, and set it up in our guest bedroom.
These are pieces that I really cherish and love to see
in my home.

Now, the most important step to refinishing your family heirlooms, or any wood for that matter, is preparing the wood. This step involves stripping off any old
finish, getting to the bare wood, repairing any dam-
ages such as nicks and missing pieces, and then
sanding the surface nice and smooth. Once prepared,
wood pieces can be decorated any number of ways—
stained or pickled, painted, stenciled or decoupaged. Eventually, a
protective sealer or finish is applied to protect your "new" piece.

> ### Simple Solution
> When it's time to apply the finish,
> the work area should be clean and
> dust-free. A card table with a sheet
> draped over and down the sides
> can make a good particle-free tent
> for your small projects.

Stripping

Quite honestly, stripping the finish off wood has to be the worst part
of any refinishing job. If the harsh chemicals and the mess aren't bad
enough, the scraping and sanding are hard work and brutal on your
hands. A lot of that has changed over the years as companies improve
and fine-tune their products, finding milder solutions that still get the
job done. Many projects are going to require that the old finish come
off and chemical stripping may be the best way to do that. The most
basic include:

TRADITIONAL CHEMICAL STRIPPERS   Of all the chemicals handled by a
do-it-yourselfer, strippers and refinishers can be the most toxic. When
using traditional chemical strippers you should always wear protective,
chemical-resistant gloves and safety goggles so you don't burn your
skin and damage your eyes. Read the labels and follow *all* safety precautions. Make sure to work in a well-ventilated area with good air circulation. If working outside, avoid direct sunlight. Always wear a respirator
recommended for use with strippers. Fumes from these paint-removing
chemicals are harmful to breathe, at best, and a common chemical used
in some strippers, methylene chloride, can be carcinogenic. A dust
mask will not protect you from these chemical fumes.

LATEX-BASED STRIPPERS   Latex-based strippers currently on the market do not contain methylene chloride. Read labels for chemical content. This new generation of strippers can be applied without special ventilation or gloves. (I wear gloves, anyway, because it will strip nail polish off in a flash!) These safer strippers do not work as fast, but that means you don't have to rush to get working with the stripper once it's on the wood. In fact, if I'm working on a piece of solid wood (*not veneer*), I usually apply a latex stripper in the evening, cover the piece with plastic, and scrape off the finish the next morning.

Using a Latex-Based Chemical Stripper

WHAT YOU NEED

Screwdriver	Paper towels
Plastic container	Medium-grade sandpaper
Stripper	Fine-grade sandpaper
Paint brush	Sanding block
Plastic spatula	Toothbrush
Refinishing pad	Twine
Chemical-resistant gloves	Safety goggles

STEP 1   Remove any hardware, doors, and drawers. Shake the stripper and apply a layer of the chemical about ⅛ in. thick over all surfaces. I pour the stripper on horizontal surfaces and then even it out with a brush. For vertical surfaces, pour the stripper into a plastic container and apply it using the brush. Always brush in the same direction, overlapping as little as possible. Latex-based strippers require anywhere from 45 minutes to 3 hours to penetrate and soften the finish. Allow enough time for the chemical to work. If the stripper dries before you have a chance to remove it, lightly mist with water using a spray bottle.

STEP 2   After letting the stripper sit for a while, test an area along the edge to see if the finish is loosened and ready to be scraped off. Note: Strippers can affect the glue in veneer pieces, so scrape the stripper off as soon as it seems ready.

Simple Solution

Use twine in the same manner as you would use dental floss to remove the finish from recessed areas on table and chair legs.

STEP 3   Scrape off the softened paint. I find that a kitchen spatula works better than a putty knife for this job because it does not have the sharp-pointed corners that can gouge or damage the surface of the wood. For carved or recessed areas, use a toothbrush or a coarse refinishing pad to lift off the stripper and finish.

STEP 4 After removing the finish, use a dampened refinishing pad to buff off the remaining residue. Wipe the surface with paper towels and allow the wood to dry.

STEP 5 Once the wood is dry, sand the piece, beginning with a medium-grade sandpaper and ending with fine-grade sandpaper (on a sanding block for flat surfaces). Note: Sand with the grain of the wood, not back and forth across the grain, as that would leave scratch marks.

Using Traditional Chemical Strippers

WHAT YOU NEED   Traditional stripper   Metal container
                Chemical-resistant gloves   Denatured alcohol
                Respirator   Steel wool
                Metal spatula   Sandpaper and sanding block
                Natural bristle paint brush   Safety goggles

STEP 1 Wearing chemical-resistant gloves, apply the stripper as described in "How to Use Latex-Based Strippers." Make sure to cover an entire surface at one time to ensure a uniform appearance. (You don't have to do an entire piece at one time, just a complete surface.) After about 8 to 10 minutes, the remover will begin to crackle. Scrape off the loosened finish immediately. Continue until the entire piece is stripped. If the stripper dries before it is scraped away, apply another coat of stripper.

STEP 2 Use denatured alcohol and steel wool to wash away the stripper residue, or follow the manufacturer's recommendations.

STEP 3 Let dry and sand.

Using a Chemical Refinisher to Remove Varnish, Lacquer, and Shellac

WHAT YOU NEED **Refinisher**
Small metal or glass container
approximately 4 in. deep

Chemical-resistant gloves
0000 steel wool pads
Safety goggles

STEP 1 Wearing chemical-resistant gloves, pour refinisher into container and dip the steel wool into the refinisher, squeezing out as much of the chemical as you can.

STEP 2 Working in an area about the size of a dinner plate, rub the dampened steel wool over the surface. Apply very light pressure as you rub the steel wool in a circular motion. Continually rinse the steel wool in the refinisher solution and change it as needed.

STEP 3 Remove any lap marks by going over them with a fresh piece of steel wool dipped in clean refinisher. Buff with the grain of the wood, using dry 0000 steel wool.

Nonchemical Stripping Options

Heat guns and sandpaper are also used to remove finishes from wood. I don't use heat guns for wood furniture, but I've used them successfully on interior doors, my garage door, and other exterior surfaces. Apply the heat just long enough to slightly blister and loosen the paint for scraping. Leaving the heat on the paint too long can cause the paint to "melt" into the grain of the wood, making it nearly impossible to remove. A heat gun with an attached Teflon™ scraper keeps the gun at a fairly safe distance and frees up your other hand. This feature definitely comes in handy when working overhead.

If the finish on wood is extremely worn, chipped, or peeling, it can be scraped with a putty knife or brass brush and sanded smooth.

Simple Solution

Pour the used refinisher into an airtight glass or metal container. Once the old finish settles to the bottom, pour the leftover refinisher into another container (you can use it again). The container can be metal or glass—no plastic—and be sure to clearly label it and keep out of the reach of children.

Simple Solution

Before applying stain or a new finish, always clean the wood's surface and make sure that no oil, dirt, grit, or residue from stripping chemicals remains. Denatured alcohol is the best raw wood cleaner and conditioner. It removes dirt and grime and neutralizes any moisture in the wood. Pour it on a clean cotton rag or cheesecloth and rub the surface in the direction of the wood grain.

Staining

Stains enable you to finish wood to match any decor without covering up its natural grain. Wood stains are available in just about any color imaginable, or you can pickle or color-wash your wood using thinned-out paint.

Even with all the options, stains basically fall into two categories:

OIL-BASED These stains give wonderfully rich colors, are absorbed by the wood without raising the grain or leaving lap marks, and are easy to apply. On the other hand, oil-based stains have strong fumes, take longer to dry, and require a solvent to clean up. And because of environmental hazards, oil-based products are not as available as they used to be.

WATER-BASED These stains have less fumes, dry quicker, clean up easier, and are less toxic, but they can raise the grain of the wood, requiring just a little more sanding. It's also a bit more difficult to achieve deep colors with water-based stains; however, by simply applying a second or third coat you can achieve rich hues.

ALL-IN-ONE STAIN AND FINISH Talk about making a project quicker and easier! The development of stain and finish all in one that the do-it-yourselfer can apply makes doing a project like this appealing to even the unhandiest among us.

General Guidelines for Applying Stain

Before using a stain, stir it well to blend the pigment. Test the color on the underside of the piece or a scrap piece of the same wood. The same stain will look different on different types of wood.

Blend stains to make the exact color you want, or lighten a stain by wiping over the freshly applied color with a mineral spirits–soaked rag. (Test this effect on scrap wood first!)

Use a brush or a clean, lint-free cloth and apply the stain from one end of the surface to the other. Avoid overlapping as much as possible. Allow the stain to penetrate the wood until it becomes slightly darker than you want the end color to be; then wipe off the excess with a dry, lint-free cloth. Leave the stain on longer or reapply for a darker shade. If the stain is too tacky to wipe off properly, put a little more on the surface, wait just a minute, and wipe it off.

Simple Solution

Stains that already have a sealer mixed in with them—known as one-step stains—need no other finish. That means one less step in staining your wood.

Do each flat surface separately. If after the stain is dry, you want a darker color, you can still apply another coat. Before applying a finish, allow the stain to dry thoroughly, per the manufacturer's recommendations.

Priming Wood

If you decide to paint rather than stain your bare wood, make sure to prime it before painting. Before priming, remove drawers, doors, and hardware. Using a good-quality painter's masking tape, mask off those areas that are not to be painted. Apply the primer to the prepared, clean surface, and when it is dry, sand the surface smooth with a fine-grade sandpaper. Then clear away the dust.

Simple Solution

Tint the primer to match the color being used for the topcoat. Your paint supplier can do this for you.

Painting Furniture

I recommend that you use enamel paint on furniture. It is self-leveling, so it won't show brush marks; also, glossy or semiglossy enamels are the most durable kinds of paints, so they'll hold up to wear and tear for years.

Prepare, prepare, prepare! Sorry, but I feel I must keep repeating how important this is (in all parts of our lives, not just do-it-yourself stuff), and believe me, I'm just as eager as the next person to save time. I've learned the hard way, though, that when you are painting with glossy enamel, if that surface has even the slightest bump, nail hole, or roughness to it, it will be magnified 100 times when this finish is applied. So, take the time to prepare the wood by using wood putty or spackle to fill imperfections and recessed nail and screw heads, to sand the surface smooth, *and* to prime it before applying the paint finish.

Place the surface you're going to paint in a horizontal position whenever possible. To paint the sides of a dresser, lay the piece on its side. Always start by painting the underside of the furniture, then the back, sides, and front, painting the top last.

Stir your paint thoroughly with a wooden stirring stick. Use long, full strokes when painting and cover the entire surface of the wood. Smooth out brush strokes with the tips of the brush. Apply the first coat against the grain of the wood, then follow the grain of the wood with the tips of the brush. Complete one surface in this manner and wait for it to dry before moving on to the next, if you are turning the piece to paint each surface in a horizontal position.

Lightly sand the surface after the first coat of paint dries. Remove the dusty residue, apply the second coat and allow it to dry completely. A clear, protective finish can follow the second coat if desired.

Simple Solution

For minor scratches on wood surfaces, there are many scratch removers available in hardware stores and home centers in different shades that make it look as if your scratch has disappeared. For deeper cuts, there are many wood-fillers available. For water rings, spread some baking soda on the stain, buff it with a damp cloth (going with the grain of the wood), wipe up the baking soda residue with a fresh cloth, and then apply a lemon oil furniture treatment.

Sealing and Finishing

There are two types of sealers:

SURFACE FINISHES   As the name implies, surface finishes stay on the top to seal and protect the wood. Paint, varnish, lacquer, shellac, and polyurethane are surface finishes.

PENETRATING FINISHES   These finishes actually sink into the wood and enhance the grain and therefore give the piece a more natural look. They cannot be applied over surface finishes. Boiled linseed oil, tung oil, Danish oil, and penetrating resins are penetrating finishes.

Which finish to use depends on the function of the piece. High-use items, such as tabletops and children's furniture, hold up better with a tough, water-resistant product like surface-finish polyurethane. Both polyurethane and penetrating-finish tung oil are good choices for durability.

Surface finishes get applied in the direction of the wood grain, using a brush. (The exception is the first coat of varnish, which is applied across grain; subsequent coats are applied with the grain of the wood.)

Apply penetrating finishes with a 100 percent cotton rag or cheese-cloth. When applying tung oil, you must rub hard to generate the heat that enables it to penetrate the surface.

Between coats, lightly sand or buff with steel wool. (I've recently started using manufactured buffing pads, also called refinishing pads, found in the paint department of most hardware stores; they don't leave behind tiny pieces of steel wool.) Remove the dust and apply another coat of sealer.

Recovering Fabric Seats

Once you've refinished the wood on your dining room chairs, you may realize that you don't want to put the faded, old fabric seats back on. You need some beautiful new fabric to set off your gorgeous refinishing job. Fortunately, it's a lot simpler to do than most people think.

If the old fabric and padding are still in good condition, you can place the new fabric over the old. Saves a lot of time! In this case, the first step is to determine the size of the replacement fabric needed. Just meas-ure from the bottom edge of one side, going up the side and then across the widest part of the chair and down the other side and add 6 in. to that measurement. Do the same going from the front of the chair to back, and again add 6 in.

Now for the fun part. Take your yardage requirements to the fabric store and look for the fabric of your dreams. Generally, you'll want to use an upholstery fabric that is designed to withstand the wear and tear of sitting. And, on your first project, you may want to avoid complex patterned fabric or stripes, because it can get real tricky trying to make sure that the pattern ends up in the same place on each chair or keeping those stripes nice and straight.

Once you have the fabric, you can follow the steps for the project below *except* leave the old fabric and padding in place, if it doesn't need replacement. If you do need to replace the padding and the old fabric is in tatters, follow all of the instructions outlined below.

How to Recover Dining Room Chairs

WHAT YOU NEED **Fabric**   **Screwdriver**
Tape measure   **Foam padding**
Scissors   **Staple gun**

STEP 1 The seats have to be removed before recovering them. After removing them (usually just a simple task of unscrewing them), remove the staples holding the existing fabric in place. Pay attention to how the corners are folded and use this same method when attaching new seat covers. Save the old fabric.

STEP 2 You can use the old fabric as the pattern for the new covers. Just cut the new fabric slightly larger and trim off any excess once it's put into place.

STEP 3 Once fabric is removed, examine the padding to determine whether it needs replacing *or* maybe you want additional padding. If so, cut a piece of padding to fit the chair seat and place it on the seat. Place the fabric right-side down on your work surface and then position padding and seat facedown on top of the fabric.

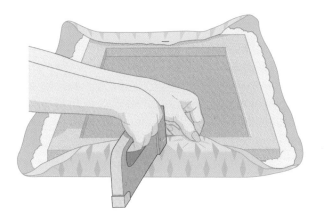

STEP 4 Staple the new seat cover to the underside of the seat in the following order: Secure the middle front first, then the middle back, pulling the fabric taut before stapling. Then secure the middle of each side.

STEP 5 Next, work from the middle of each side to within 3 in. of the corners, stapling the fabric every couple of inches (you can come back and add more staples as needed after all sides are secured in position) and in from the edge of the seat about 1 in. Check every once in a while to see that the pattern remains centered.

STEP 6 Fold, tuck, and staple the cover in the corners in the same manner as they were folded in the old seat cover. (This is similar to neatly wrapping a package.) Reduce bulk by cutting away any excess fabric. Reinstall seat.

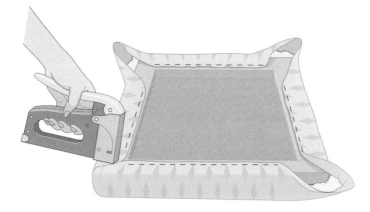

The Boxing Ring

As I worked with wood over the years, it became very clear that if I could perfect making a "box" it would greatly simplify making many projects. For instance, picture frames, bed frames, under-the-bed storage units, headboards, cabinets, flower boxes, shelving units, hanging pot racks—you get the idea—all became easier once I knew how to make a box out of wood.

Of course, not all boxes are the same. Some have backs or bottoms (e.g., shelving units, bed frames, and flower boxes); others have backs and doors (e.g., cabinets and toy chests); while still others have only the four sides (e.g., picture frames and pot racks). Some are shallow, while others are deep, some low and wide, others tall and narrow, some end up horizontal, others standing, some attach to walls, others are free-standing. Some boxes even lie on their backs. Whew!

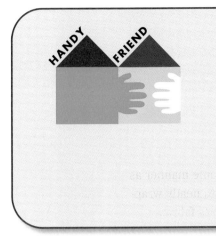

Kelly Riordian, editor-in-chief of special publications for Hearst Publishing, where she works on a number of special editions of *House Beautiful* and *Good Housekeeping*, gives you some pointers on keeping your furniture clean:

- When vacuuming your floors, take the time to vacuum your furniture, too. Just use the upholstery attachment on your vacuum cleaner.
- Before using a store-bought cleanser or polish on your furniture, make sure you know how it will interact with the wood or fabric. If you don't know, you'll need to spot-test cleansers on a hidden piece of the furniture.

Despite the mind-boggling possibilities on the theme, making a good box boils down to one thing: becoming proficient at joining corners. Some of those corners will be mitered and then joined, others will be straight cut and joined flush. Both approaches will lead to a square corner.

Take it from me, *always* use a good wood glue and clamp the joints until they dry; wood glue expands as it dries, and the joints become loose in no time! It's worth the money to invest in a set of four corner clamps if you are planning to do much woodworking. If you don't have clamps, you can nail or screw the joints to hold them secure as the glue dries (in some cases, I do this even though I have clamps). The nails and screws become the clamps. Small finishing nails work fine for mitered corners, and screws or nails will do for flush joints. Be sure to drill pilot holes no matter which you use, otherwise the wood will probably split because it's so close to the end. In fact, many times I glue *and* nail or screw even if I'm also using clamps.

Simple Solution

If you're working with wood and find yourself with leftover pieces of baseboards, crown molding, or shoe molding, you can use them to make picture frames.

My final advice: Don't be too hard on yourself if the corners are not perfect—that's what sandpaper, wood putty, and spackling compound are for. And remember that practice makes perfect (or *almost* perfect). The mail organizer project below is a great one to cut your teeth on. (Also, check out the cornice project on page 80.)

Did I Get Any Mail?

How many times does an important letter or bill get waylaid between your mailbox and your desk? Here's something that looks good and is handy: a wooden mail organizer. Using a system of dividers in place, you can use the organizer to separate the mail by family member, or you can use the organizer to sort your own mail. For example, one slot could be for bills, another for personal letters, or a third for donation requests or junk mail. You decide—it's your mail!

Different sizes of this same organizer could be used all over the house—under the bed as storage, on the desk to sort papers, and in the closet to keep your clothes in order.

How to Make a Mail Organizer

WHAT YOU NEED **Four pieces of wood planks**
(cut to size)
Wood glue
Nails or screws

Two pieces of wood for dividers
Clamps
Drill and bits
Safety glasses

STEP 1 Cut sides, top, and bottom to desired size. If you are going to stain the piece, I find it works best to do that before joining the box together. If I want it painted, I usually paint after it's made.

STEP 2 Stand the two sides upright and position top flush with sides. Drill pilot holes for nails or screws (use countersink bit for screws). Run a bead of glue along the edges of sides, reposition top, and secure with nails or screws. Turn upside down and repeat to attach bottom to sides.

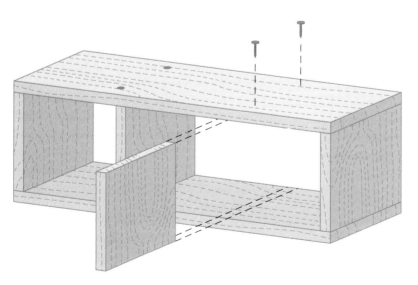

STEP 3 For the back (you can use a piece of luan cut to size), lay it in position on the box frame and drill pilot holes all the way around (about every 3 in. to 4 in.), remove the back, and run a bead of glue around the box frame and then glue the back piece on. Nail and/or clamp it tight.

STEP 4 Install dividers with glue and insert nails for more stability. If you have a router, you may want to put in removable dividers by carving grooves in the top and bottom of the box before assembly; just remember that, since the dividers will be going "into" the wood, you want them slightly taller than the ones you would glue into place.

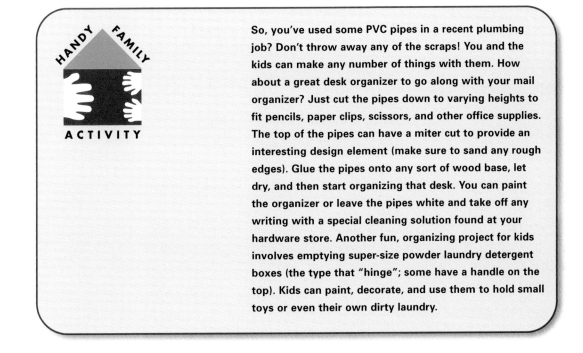

HANDY FAMILY
ACTIVITY

So, you've used some PVC pipes in a recent plumbing job? Don't throw away any of the scraps! You and the kids can make any number of things with them. How about a great desk organizer to go along with your mail organizer? Just cut the pipes down to varying heights to fit pencils, paper clips, scissors, and other office supplies. The top of the pipes can have a miter cut to provide an interesting design element (make sure to sand any rough edges). Glue the pipes onto any sort of wood base, let dry, and then start organizing that desk. You can paint the organizer or leave the pipes white and take off any writing with a special cleaning solution found at your hardware store. Another fun, organizing project for kids involves emptying super-size powder laundry detergent boxes (the type that "hinge"; some have a handle on the top). Kids can paint, decorate, and use them to hold small toys or even their own dirty laundry.

Wicker Gone Wrong

There's no reason you have to get rid of wicker furniture just because some of its wicker has gone astray. Repair can be as simple as reattaching loose pieces and replacing broken strands. Wicker strands, which are referred to as "wickerwork" or basketry, are available at woodworking supply stores. Rattan is probably the most common type of wicker work. Soak the strands in hot water for 15 to 20 minutes before beginning repairs to make the rattan pliable.

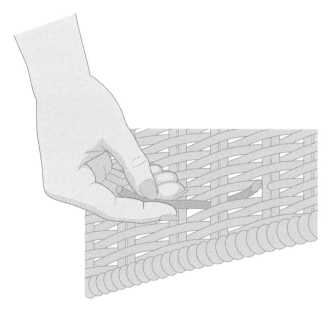

REPAIRING DAMAGED WOVEN WICKER   Work from underneath. Snip out the damaged material with wire cutters, making sure the cut end remaining on the chair is secured under a crossing piece. Cut a new piece about 2 in. longer than the old one (because the wicker will shrink as it dries). Start weaving from the underside 1 in. before the repair section, pulling the wicker tight as you work. Weave, following the pattern. Use needle-nose pliers to help pull the wicker strands through if necessary. Apply Quicktite™, a gel-type superglue (this is the only glue I know of that will bond damp surfaces), to each end. Press the ends in place, using tweezers or a toothpick, and hold for about 30 seconds or until the adhesive grabs.

REPAIRING WRAPPED WICKER   Some furniture pieces have wicker wrapped around certain areas, such as the legs and arms of a chair or the legs of a dresser. Repairing "wrap" can be as easy as simply rewrapping and securing.

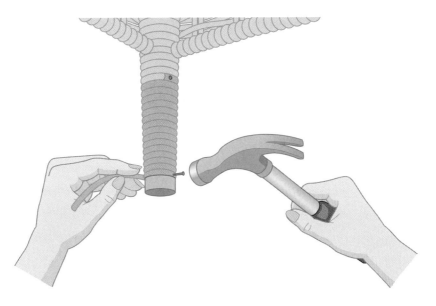

If the wicker is damaged, cut off the old piece and replace it with a new wrapping. Use wire cutters or scissors to cut the wicker. Apply the gel superglue to the loose end of the existing wrapped wicker on the leg and secure with a ½ in. brad. Then apply the superglue to the end of the damp replacement wrap and tack it in place using a ½ in. brad. The ends of the old and new rattan should butt together. Wind the new piece around the leg tightly and evenly, applying the superglue occasionally. Tuck the end under the final turn of wrapped wicker. Apply the gel superglue and tack the end in place with a brad. Use wire cutters to snip the end off so that it's flush.

CLEANING WICKER   Clean wicker with a soft paintbrush or toothbrush and soapy water and rinse. Sunlight will make wicker shrink, so if the piece needs tightening up, let it dry in the sun, otherwise in the shade.

If you're planning to paint wicker furniture, spray painting will be the most efficient and effective method (see page 37 for directions).

What's in Store

The projects outlined in this chapter will definitely make your home *feel* like your own. Of course, you want to live in a house that not only looks good, but *feels* good as well. In the next chapter, we'll look at how easy it is to make sure the air and temperature are right throughout the household. And, for those times when only fresh air will do, we'll look at ways that you can make your yard truly special for family gatherings. So, say goodbye to nasty drafts and overheated living rooms and say hello to coziness and comfort both inside and outside the home.

PLAY IT SAFE!

- Before pressing an old antique chair into use, make sure that its legs and seat are secure and won't buckle under weight.

- Carefully sand all wood surfaces smooth so you won't get splinters.

- Use stripping chemicals only in a well-ventilated area.

- Keep stripping compounds out of reach of children and pets.

- If you're a single woman living alone, avoid hanging accents on your door, doorbell, or mailbox that might send that signal to potential intruders.

Around the Home

11

I've never been one to spend a lot of time worrying about having a picture-perfect home that was all gussied up for entertaining (especially when the children were young), nor did I have fancy-filled dreams of its being captured in a glossy home magazine. In fact, my kids would often tell me how happy they were that our house was so relaxed and comfortable, where they could bring their friends without fear of breaking a valuable knick-knack. That was music to my ears!

In my experience, one of the most important steps to making a house comfy-cozy inside is keeping room temperatures comfortable and draft-free and making the outside inviting as well. In this chapter, I'll show you not only how to install a programmable thermostat but also how to make a tranquil water fountain for your yard. Comfy, cozy, and do-it-yourself are the key themes here.

Room Temperature

Why settle for being too hot or too cold when you can be just right? A programmable thermostat is a great way to modulate the room temperature *and* reduce your heating and air-conditioning bills by as much as 20 to 30 percent. Just program the thermostat to raise or lower the temperature (depending on the time of year) when everyone is asleep, when family members are usually home, and when they're not.

There are many different types of thermostats, not only in style and function, but also for the different types of heating and air-conditioning systems. Make sure you know what type of system you have before you go to the store to buy a new thermostat.

How to Install a Programmable Thermostat

WHAT YOU NEED   **Thermostat**   **Pencil**   **Masking tape**
                Screwdriver   **Drill**   **Batteries**
                Safety glasses

STEP 1   As with all electrical projects, shut off the power to the furnace/thermostat at your main power box. Remove old thermostat. Every thermostat is different, so you'll need to look for all the screws and plates on your particular model.

STEP 2   Once the top is removed, you'll need to remove another series of screws that hold the wiring plate to the wall.

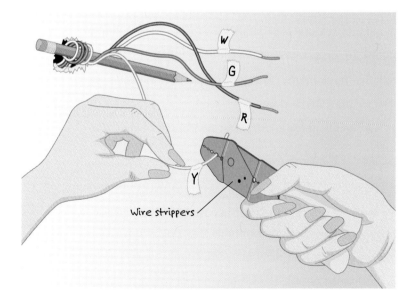

STEP 3   Disconnect the wires from the screw terminals. Generally, the wires will be color coded: the yellow wire is connected to the screw labeled with a "Y," the white to the "W," the red to the "R," and green to the "G." Now, if your wires do not have colored insulation, *or if the wires are colored but not connected according to color,* undo them one at a time and place a piece of masking tape on each wire and mark its matching connection. For example, put a "W" on the masking tape attached to the wire that was connected to the "W" screw, regardless of the wire's color.

STEP 4   You don't want the wires to fall back into the wall, so tape the wires onto the wall or wrap them around a pencil. Remove the mounting plate. Just remember to retape the wires to the wall (or rewrap) when you discard the plate.

STEP 5   If your new mounting plate holes do not match up to the old ones, you'll have to redrill holes and secure your screws with anchors. Install the plate.

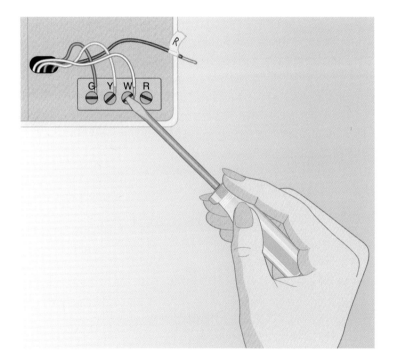

STEP 6   Reconnect the wires and carefully push the excess wire back into the wall cavity. Attach the thermostat, and make sure you've put in the batteries so it stays programmed just in case there's a power outage.

Stop Those Leaks

Air leaking in and out of our homes can cost us an awful lot of money in heating and air-conditioning. The best way to stop those leaks from the exterior of the house is with caulk. Caulk comes in many different colors and some can be painted. Just make sure you buy the right type for your needs. After laying a bead of caulk, you want to smooth it out by running a damp finger over it.

Windows, obviously, are leaky culprits. If you can fit a dime between the sash and the windowsill, install some reusable weather stripping. It's made out of a rubbery substance: Most come in the shape of a tube with a fin. The "fin" just gets squeezed into the crack to stop the leak. But for really bad leaks, try some of those plastic-window-insulator kits. Basically, you put double-sided tape around the perimeter of the window, attach plastic sheets, and then shrink the plastic tight with a hair dryer.

For leaks around doors, weather stripping will save you a lot of money. There is a variety of weather stripping out there; the more expensive ones generally last longer. Also, for leaks under the door, install a door sweep. There are self-adhesive ones as well as screw-ons. Decorative draft dodgers also work, but only when you're home to put them into place.

Simple Solution

Believe it or not, about 10 percent of air infiltration is through outlets and switches. Stop those drafts by removing switch and outlet covers (turn off the electricity at the main power box first!) and tracing the shape onto craft foam. Cut the foam shape out and place the foam sealers behind the covers on all outside walls and unheated rooms such as garages and attics. And while you're doing this project, you may want to label the back of your switch and outlet plates so you can match them with their proper circuit breakers. Number the plate with the corresponding circuit number on the breaker box. I also tape a list inside the breaker with exactly what is on each circuit: for example, "kitchen light switch" on south wall, "dining room outlet" on north wall, and so forth, because many times a breaker will not control an entire room.

How to Make a Decorative Draft Dodger

WHAT YOU NEED   **Fabric** (size depends on door size)
Dried beans, sand, or doll-making beads

STEP 1   Cut a piece of fabric 4 in. wide and 4 in. longer than the width of your door.

STEP 2   Fold right sides together lengthwise and sew a ¼ in. seam along one short end and down both long sides.

STEP 3   Turn the tube right side out and fill it with dried beans, sand, or doll-making beads.

STEP 4   Hand-stitch the open end and place it by the door to block drafts.

In the Yard

Americans certainly love their yards. In his book, *Crabgrass Frontier* (Oxford University Press, 1987), Kenneth T. Jackson says that between 1825 and 1875 many Americans stopped needing to use their yards to grow food, giving them more freedom to do other things with their lawns. And with the invention of the first lawn mower in 1831, Americans started replacing their rough meadowlike grass with neatly manicured lawns. However, early Americans generally did not use their backyards for fun and relaxation. In fact, Jackson says, yards back then were "typically rancid, disreputable, and overrun by rodents. Regular garbage collection was rare before the Civil War, and most families threw their refuse out the doors to scavenging dogs and pigs." Just imagine what your neighbors would say if you started doing that!

Luckily, our neighbors are basically responsible and we're all free to enjoy our yards. One great way to do that is by adding on a patio or deck—which can be an integral part of a home and the family's life. I know it is for my family. We fire up the grill and have family cookouts all summer long. It's also a great place to just relax and take a few moments to stop and smell the roses.

Instructions below show you how to dry-lay a walkway, and you can use the same technique to create a patio. Obviously, you'll just be working on a larger area.

How to Build a Brick Walkway

WHAT YOU NEED   Bricks

Stakes and string

Tamper

Edging

Dry coarse sand (not play sand!)

Circular saw

Mason's brick set

Chalk

Broom

Spray paint

Flat-bladed shovel

Landscape cloth

#9 Road-grade gravel

Notched screed board

Masonry blade

Small sledgehammer

Bricklayer's hammer (optional)

Safety glasses

STEP 1   Preparation takes the most time (as usual). Plan the dimensions of the walkway. In mapping these out, try to keep the cutting of bricks to a minimum by factoring their size into your calculations. Also, plan out the pattern you'd like to create with your bricks (i.e., in a running line with the path, running across the path, or at an angle in a herringbone design). Then mark the designated area on your lawn with spray paint and stake string along the outer edges.

STEP 2   Remove sod and dirt down to about 6 in. to 8 in. (depending on the thickness of your brick) using a flat-bladed shovel. Slope slightly away from the house to provide drainage.

STEP 3   If you don't want vegetation growing between the bricks, cover the area with landscape cloth. Install edging to contain path or patio and pour a layer of coarse gravel to a depth of about 2 in. Cover gravel with landscape cloth and cover that with about 2 in. of sand (the amount of gravel and sand depends on how deep you dug and how thick your pavers are). Tamp the entire area to make a solid base and level it using a notched screed board, shuffling it back and forth from side to side.

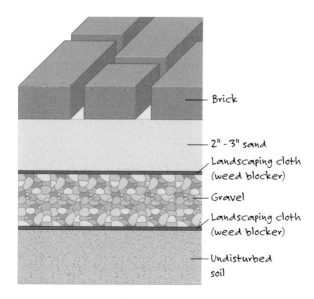

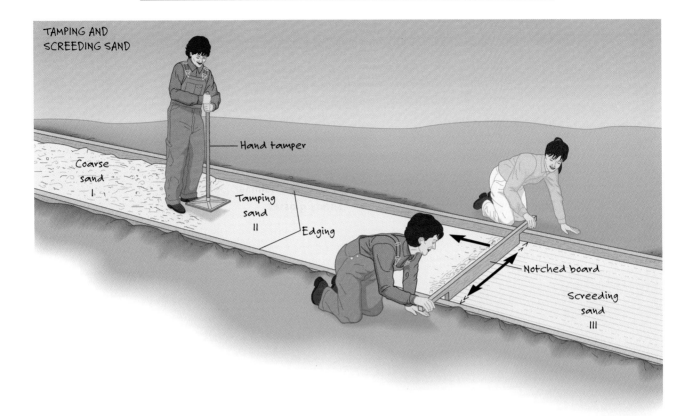

TAMPING AND SCREEDING SAND

Coarse sand I

Hand tamper

Tamping sand II

Edging

Notched board

Screeding sand III

STEP 4 If you are doing a straight path of equal width throughout, you can cut all bricks at the same time. Using chalk, mark the cut lines all around the brick. Use a circular saw with masonry blade or a mason's brick set and small sledgehammer to score and break. Knock off any jagged edges with a bricklayer's hammer.

STEP 5 Lay the bricks in place in accordance with your preplanned bricklaying design.

STEP 6 Spread sand across the surface of the brick and sweep into spaces between the bricks. Wait a few days and repeat until all the gaps are filled.

Your Private Eden

If you think fountains are only for fancy courtyards and enchanted gardens, think again. There's no reason why you can't have your very own fountain bubbling gently in your backyard. Just set up a chaise lounge alongside, grab a great book, and you have the perfect recipe for a relaxing afternoon!

HANDY FAMILY ACTIVITY

Make a flag to fly outside your patio or porch using nylon fabric (just tell your fabric store salesperson you're making a flag, and he or she will point you in the right direction). This is an activity that kids of all ages will enjoy. To make flags using your children's design, just take their drawing and have it photocopied to the size you want it on the flag. Then cut out the backing nylon fabric, hem edges, and sew an open-ended hem (pocket) for the pole. Cut out the pieces of the design, attach them to the backing fabric with fusible webbing, and set them using an iron. You also can hem the edges of the flag using fusible tape, so that the fabric doesn't fray.

You can make your fountain as simple or as elaborate as you like. One time, I took a huge, plastic, clay-colored saucer and placed a fairly large clay pot upside-down on top of it. Starting with that base, it then was just a matter of creating a tower of different-sized pots with saucers on top of them to form plateaus for the water to travel downward from saucer to saucer and finally into the bottom container. I also had to file notches in the saucers' lips, so the water could spill to the next level, and drill a series of holes through the containers to allow the water tubing to pass through. (Directions follow.)

Once you've established your fountain base, it's time to bring it to life with special accents. Try rocks or shells or maybe even candles on the top level (where they won't get wet). Flowers and colorful water plants also bring life to your fountain.

For a simple fountain you need:

- A base to contain the water (you can purchase small, medium, and large premolded plastic garden ponds)
- A submersible pump with an attachment that shoots the water into the air so it falls back into the container
- Simple decorations, such as water plants or flowers

This is the simplest and least expensive installation that still has the pleasing look and sound of a fountain.

For a more elaborate fountain you could use:

- A barrel as base container
- A submersible pump
- A watering can for the fountain's spout
- Decorative flowering plants

Place the pump in the container submerged in water, attach a tube that will pump the water into a hole in the bottom of a watering can, which is tilted as if pouring water into the barrel. (The watering can is attached to the side of the barrel.) When the can fills, the water will eventually come out of the spout of the can—as if watering your flowers.

The following fountain can be used indoors or out.

How to Make a Clay-Pot Fountain

WHAT YOU NEED
Submersible pump	Clay saucers
Clay pots	Round file and/or rotary tool
Clear acrylic spray	with grinding stone bit
Drill	Wood spacers or blocks
Masonry drill bit	Silicone sealant
Scissors	Safety glasses

STEP 1   Gather up several different-sized clay pots and saucers to be stacked in succession, so that when the water flows down, it slides in tiers over the pots. Three tiers makes a nice fountain, but you can make it any size you want—two, three, or more. You just need the base container to be large enough in diameter to hold all the pots and tall enough to hold sufficient water to submerge the pump.

STEP 2   Lay out the design.

STEP 3   If the base you choose is porous (clay), spray it with a clear acrylic sealer to waterproof it. Let it dry.

STEP 4   A notch is needed in each saucer's edge to direct the water to the next lower one. Soak the saucers in water for at least an hour to make them easier to drill and file. (Also soak the bottom of the pot that the tube will thread through if the drain hole is smaller than the tube.)

STEP 5   Now, you have to set the pump on the base. Take the largest pot (6 in. to 8 in.) and file four notches along the upper edge (you can use a rotary tool with a grinding stone). This is the pot that will be turned upside down, concealing the pump. One notch is to accommodate the electrical cord, and the others are to allow water under the pot.

STEP 6 Turn the pot upside down, thread the pump tubing through the hole in the bottom of the pot (you may need to make the hole larger), and set it into position. Allow excess tubing to extend out of the top.

STEP 7 Using a masonry drill bit, drill a hole the same size as the tube, in the center of the saucer that goes on top of the first pot.

STEP 8 Thread the tubing through the saucer and trim it to about ½ in. above the saucer.

STEP 9 Seal any gaps between the tubing and saucer with waterproof sealant and let it cure. Place a small inverted saucer over the end of the tube to conceal it. (Make three or four notches in this saucer before putting it in place.)

STEP 10 Stack the remaining pots with a saucer on top of each in a tiered pattern inside the base. All these saucers need notches about ½ in. to ¾ in. deep; when you are arranging the tiers, the notch on the upper tiers should be placed over the next lower saucer.

STEP 11 Fill the base saucer with enough water to cover the pump (no higher than within about ⅜ in. from the top of the base) and then plug in the pump. Here's what happens: Water is pumped from the base up the tube through the upside-down pot into the top saucer. When that saucer fills with water it will overflow the notch to the next lower saucer, that one will overflow its notch to the next, and then back into the base.

Simple Solution

If your garden hose has sprung a leak, it's easy to repair. All you have to do is cut out the damaged part (in other words, you *will* split the hose in two), then buy a simple repair kit that will join the two pieces back together. Insert the connector from the kit into each cut end and tighten the clamp to hold it in place. If you have trouble getting the connector into the hose, just wipe some liquid soap on the connector and it should slide right in.

Don't Be Left in the Gutter

Gutters and downspouts keep rainwater and melting snow from running off the roof directly to the ground around the foundation of your home, seeping through the foundation and into the basement or crawl space. Imagine the cleanup that would require! Actually the gutters and downspouts collect and direct the water away from the house.

So, instead of worrying about cleaning up a flooded home, make sure to maintain the gutters and downspouts. Your time and effort will depend on what they are made of and how many trees you have around your home.

Your hands are the best tools for this task. Wear heavy work gloves, because there can be sharp thorns, twigs, and who knows what else mixed in those leaves. Don't use sharp tools to scoop out the muck, because you can accidentally damage your gutter. If you need a little help getting some of the debris out, use a plastic-coated kitchen spatula or a plastic scoop. After you've cleared everything, rinse the gutters out with a hose. And don't get rid of those leaves so fast; throw them in your compost bin if you have one.

Simple Solution

We all know that webbed lawn furniture eventually comes undone from wear and tear. What damaged our chairs the most was throwing them in and out of the car trunk for use at kids' baseball and soccer games. After almost falling through one, I decided it was time to take action. The frames were in great condition. All we needed to do was remove the damaged webbing, weave in a new piece, and then screw it into place. Make sure to cut the new piece longer than the old one, because you'll fold the edges into triangles and then screw it into place. Those triangles give it needed reinforcement (so you don't take a spill in the eighth inning).

What's in Store

Obviously in this chapter and others, I've shown you some projects that have involved working with and around electricity. I know that, when I first started doing projects and working on bare wires and such, I was a bit more nervous than doing something like hanging a roman shade. Even some of the most confident do-it-yourselfers I know shy away from projects with the slightest bit of wattage involved. But, I promise, electrical projects don't have to be so scary. There's a big difference between having a healthy fear of electricity and being intimidated by it.

By reading the next chapter, you'll understand the basics and then you can make an educated decision about doing it yourself or bringing in a professional electrician.

Electricity doesn't have to be a foreign language.

PLAY IT
SAFE!

- If your dog stays out in a yard with a chain-link fence, make sure to post a warning to strangers to keep their hands to themselves.

- Keep your home's climate at a temperature that's appropriate for the health needs of both your youngest and oldest family members.

- Teach your children the rules of the road: Make sure they know to look both ways before crossing the streets near your home.

- Monitor your children's play in the backyard.

- If you have a pool, make sure to keep the gate locked and the pool covered when not in use and supervise children's use of it. Consider adding a special motion sensor for the pool—the sensor will sound a loud alarm when it detects a preset amount of movement of the water.

Wired ¹²

Imagine that your teenager is in the bathroom and she's waiting for her 600-watt curling iron to warm up while she dries her hair with a 1200-watt blow dryer in front of a 500-watt illuminated mirror. She wants to listen to music, so she turns on the radio.

But instead of hearing songs by her favorite rock group, she hears the pop of your 15-amp circuit with the 1800-watt limit. She's overloaded the circuit!

If you experience blown fuses or tripped circuit breakers frequently, or if you have electrical service less than 100 amps, you should consider hiring a qualified licensed electrician to upgrade your home's electricity. But not all electrical problems require you to hire someone.

Even if the thought of doing electrical repairs scares the wits out of you, in this chapter I'm going to show you some really easy do-it-yourself repair projects.

Electricity 101

But first, here's a little primer on electricity for you. Electricity is carried to your home in cables made of heavy-duty multistrand wires. These can be found above or below ground. The electricity's first stop is your home's electrical meter. From there, it goes to your fuse or circuit breaker box. (In this book, we've referred to this box as the main power box.)

From the main power box, the electricity is carried through your home on insulated wires. The wires distributing electricity throughout your home are called hot wires; the wires returning to the main power box are referred to as neutral. When you turn on a radio, plug in a clock, or heat an electric oven, the electricity doesn't stop at the appliance. Rather, it works in a nonstop circular pattern—going from the main box to your appliance and back to the main box, and this keeps happening until you turn your appliance off.

Before working on any electrical projects, there are certain safety precautions you must take. If you're working on wires attached to the home, you want to shut off their electrical current at the main power box. If you're working on an individual appliance, make sure to unplug it.

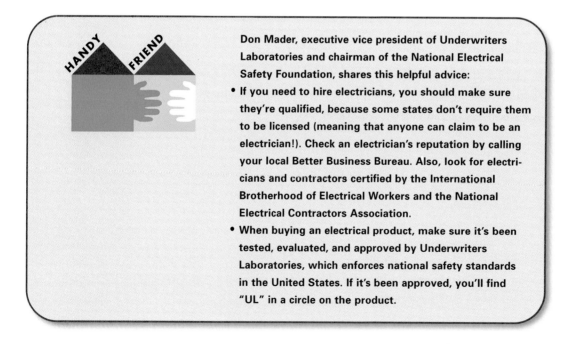

HANDY FRIEND

Don Mader, executive vice president of Underwriters Laboratories and chairman of the National Electrical Safety Foundation, shares this helpful advice:

- If you need to hire electricians, you should make sure they're qualified, because some states don't require them to be licensed (meaning that anyone can claim to be an electrician!). Check an electrician's reputation by calling your local Better Business Bureau. Also, look for electricians and contractors certified by the International Brotherhood of Electrical Workers and the National Electrical Contractors Association.

- When buying an electrical product, make sure it's been tested, evaluated, and approved by Underwriters Laboratories, which enforces national safety standards in the United States. If it's been approved, you'll find "UL" in a circle on the product.

"Is It Plugged In?"

In my first home, I had a dishwasher that had to be about 20 years old when it went on the fritz. For several months, I had managed to get it going with an occasional hard shove on the door. But eventually, that didn't even work. So, I gave in and bought a new one.

I decided to install it myself. My father told me it was simple to do. It is simple, but what I realized when I began removing the old dishwasher was that I didn't even need a new one. You see, when I removed the front panel of the old dishwasher, I saw a dangling wire. A lightbulb went on in my head! All I needed to do was reconnect that wire to get the electrical system going again. I found where the wire belonged, connected it, and flipped the circuit breaker back on, and, lo and behold, the old dishwasher was new again.

It took some talking, but I was able to convince the appliance store salesman to take back the new dishwasher for a full refund.

Stripping Wire Insulation

Many basic repairs assume that you know how to properly strip wires. So let's start there.

Preset your wire strippers so that the notched opening equals the diameter of the wire. Score the insulation around the wire by closing the jaws of the stripper around the wire; open and close the stripper as you turn the wire. Then, holding the stripper jaws at the score line, close the handles, push the tool away with one hand as you hold the wire with the other.

Simple Solution

If you're a beginner at stripping wires, buy some wire (it's sold by the foot at your local hardware store) and practice before starting a project.

WARNING **Be careful to score only the insulation and not the wire. Cutting off strands of stranded wire, or denting, nicking, or compressing solid wire can damage it and cause it to overheat and start a fire!**

HANDY FAMILY ACTIVITY

As you learn about electricity, why not take this time to teach your children about how it works and why they need to be careful around it? Of course, make sure they understand the importance of never using electrical appliances around water, and remind them to shut the lights off whenever they leave a room. Tell them this not only saves money but protects the environment as well.

Electrical Plugs

Now, here are some easy directions for replacing plugs. The three most commonly used plugs are light-duty, polarized, and three-prong grounded. Don't be embarrassed to bring your old plug with you to the hardware store so you're sure to buy the right replacement. (There are times I still take parts with me, especially if I'm doing a project for the first time.)

How to Replace a Snap-On Plug
(light duty) (no wire stripping necessary)

WHAT YOU NEED **Replacement plug**
Wire cutters

STEP 1   This type of plug is for light duty, generally used on lamps. Unplug the lamp. Using the wire cutters or the scissors area of your needle-nose pliers, cut straight across the zip cord just above the old plug and throw it out.

STEP 2   Open the replacement plug by lifting its lever. Push the end of the cord that was cut into the slot as far as it will go and snap the cover closed. When the cover is closed securely, metal teeth inside the plug bite through the insulation to make contact with the wire and act as an electrical conduit. (This is just one of several types of light-duty plugs; check out the others at the hardware store.)

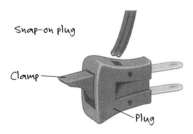

Snap-on plug

Clamp

Plug

How to Replace a Quick Plug (light duty) (no wire stripping necessary)

WHAT YOU NEED **Replacement plug**
Wire cutters

STEP 1 Unplug the lamp. Cut across the zip cord just above the plug you're replacing, using your wire cutters or needle-nose pliers. Discard the old plug.

STEP 2 The core of the replacement plug is attached to prongs. To remove the core, pinch the prongs together and pull it out.

STEP 3 Spread the prongs open and thread the zip cord through the top of the plug and into the core as far as it will go. Squeeze the prongs back together tightly. Like other light-duty plugs, this plug contains metal teeth that make the connection between the wire and the electric current.

How to Replace a Screw-Terminal Polarized Plug

WHAT YOU NEED **Polarized replacement plug**   **Slotted screwdriver**
Needle-nose pliers   **Wire strippers**

STEP 1 Unplug the appliance. Cut off the old plug using needle-nose pliers.

STEP 2 Use a slotted screwdriver to separate the cover from the core of the new plug and slip the cord through the hole in the top of the plug cover and out the bottom.

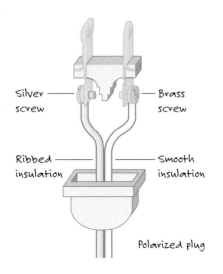

Silver screw — Brass screw

Ribbed insulation — Smooth insulation

Polarized plug

Simple Solution

It's easy to spot a polarized plug. One of its prongs is larger than the other; frequently when you try to plug it into an outlet, it won't fit, and you have to turn it around the other way.

STEP 3 Split the cord for about 2 in. along the seam that unites the two insulated wires. For some plugs: Tie the two ends together in an Underwriters knot (see page 98 for directions), and then strip about ½ in. of the insulation off the ends of both wires using wire strippers.

STEP 4 Push the plug down against the Underwriters knot so that it slips into the body of the plug. (For the plug shown, there isn't room for an Underwriters knot; as the core is pushed into the cover the cord gets wedged in position, securing it in place.)

STEP 5 A polarized plug has one brass and one silver screw terminal; it needs to be wired a certain way. Take a close look at the cord insulation around the wires: one will be ribbed, the other smooth. The wire in the ribbed insulation is the "neutral" wire and gets connected to the silver terminal and the one in the smooth insulation is the hot wire and gets connected to the brass terminal. To make the connections, gently twist the tiny strands of wire together, turning the strands on each end in a **clockwise** direction. Wrap the end of each wire around the appropriate screw terminal in a clockwise direction and tighten the screws down over the wires.

STEP 6 Snap the cover over the core of the plug.

How to Replace a Three-Prong Plug

WHAT YOU NEED **Replacement plug**   **Slotted screwdriver**
Needle-nose pliers   **Wire cutters**

STEP 1 Unplug the appliance. Cut off the old plug. Three-prong plugs contain three terminals instead of two—one brass, one silver, and one green. The ground wire will either be bare copper or it will have green insulation. Thread the cord through the new three-prong plug. When making the Underwriters knot, do not include the grounding wire.

STEP 2 Strip the outer insulation back about 2 in., being careful not to damage the wires' insulation on the inside. Tie an Underwriters knot and strip about ½ in. insulation from all three wires (see pages 98-99). Connect the ground wire to the green ground screw, white insulated wire (neutral) to the silver terminal, and black (hot) wire to the brass terminal (wrap the wires in a clockwise direction around the screw). Replace the insulated cover.

Many changes, repairs, or enhancements to your electrical system *will* require the work of a licensed electrician. Put your family's safety first; know your limitations and don't hesitate to bring in professional help when needed.

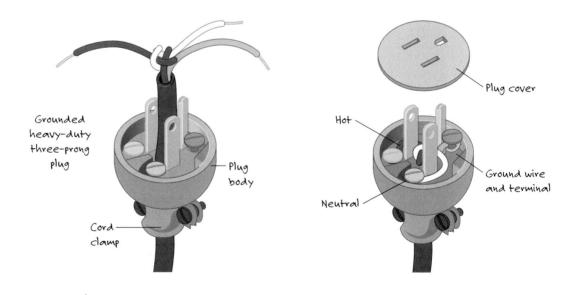

Grounded
heavy-duty
three-prong
plug

Plug
body

Cord
clamp

Plug cover

Hot

Ground wire
and terminal

Neutral

PLAY IT SAFE!

- Place child-guard caps over electrical outlets.

- Make sure your children understand that they should not insert fingers or any objects other than plugs into outlets.

- Always unplug an appliance by grasping a plug rather than by pulling on its cord.

- If an appliance is not used frequently, keep it unplugged with its cord neatly stowed.

- A bunch of loose, plugged-in cords can be dangerous—not to mention unsightly. The problem is easy to take care of. Just wrap and secure a plastic electrical tie around the group of cords every 8 in. or so. (Loose cords have become more of a problem with the addition of VCRs, computers, faxes, and so much other electronic equipment in our homes.)

- Always turn off the circuit and use a voltage tester to make sure that the electrical current is off, before attempting any electrical work. (See page 92 for instructions on how to use a voltage tester.)

Safe and Sound

Our desire to have a safe and secure home is as old as the Ice Age. There's evidence that, back then, people would take animal bones and stack them together to form a wall around their area so that enemy tribes could not get in. Later, there were moats built around castles. And today, we're still trying to protect our castles, although the way we protect them has changed.

It took a close call to get me to pay more attention to home security issues. One night, a burglar jimmied the spring lock on one of our neighbors' doors and stole many of their valuable possessions and irreplaceable heirlooms. Luckily no one was home at the time, and no one was hurt. But it did get my attention. From that point, I made it my business to do as much as possible to make our home more secure. Dead bolts and window locks were the most obvious additions. Even though I realize there is no way you can guarantee your safety, these measures do make me feel better.

Crime-Wise

Each year, one in five homeowners in the United States is the victim of a burglary. And it is said that, in the next 20 years, three out of four homes will be broken into. The FBI reports that intruders take an average of $1,000 in property. And get this: More than 50 percent of the time, the intruders return to the scene of the crime. They've already cased your home on the first trip and know what's left to take, plus they figure you're so traumatized over the first break-in that your guard is down.

Though you can't prevent crime, you can take steps to deter the criminal's efforts. Consider making the following security improvements in and around your home.

Simple Solution

Live by the age-old adage: "Better safe than sorry."

- Install dead bolt locks on all entry doors, including attached garages and basements.
- Put locking hardware on ground-floor windows and any others that are easily accessible.
- If your neighborhood has a moderate-to-high crime rate, consider adding protective metal screens or bars to your street-level doors and windows. Also, you might want to take the same precautions for any doors or windows opening onto a fire escape or courtyard.
- Add a peephole so you know who's at the door before opening it.
- Mount motion-detecting lights around the perimeter of your home and within your home.
- Eliminate places where intruders can hide by trimming shrubbery and hedges around the doors and windows.
- Install timers on lamps, radios, and other appliances so that they go on and off throughout your home at random times.

Simple Solution

Vary your daily routine so potential intruders can't track your whereabouts.

I also think that you can pick up some good ideas by talking to your neighbors about the type of security precautions they feel are needed in your vicinity—especially if you're a newcomer to the neighborhood.

Weather-Wise

Protecting ourselves from intruders is an important consideration, but our home's entries must also be weatherproof and resistant to the elements. So we'll keep factors such as insulation and seals in mind, as we walk through the options for doors and windows.

Doors

Though doors come in a wide variety of styles, there are several factors other than looks to consider when purchasing one. A good door will be secure and weatherproof. Steel doors, of course, are the strongest and most durable. Many also feature a core of polyurethane foam that helps to soundproof and insulate your home.

In wooden doors, a solid core offers strength and durability. Hollow-core wooden doors are not suitable for exterior use: they simply are not strong enough.

Simple Solution

If you want the strength of a steel door without the cost, nail a metal lip to the edge of your wooden door.

Locking Hardware

Hardware provides another level of security. Don't skimp here. A simple spring lock (such as what you'd find on a bathroom door) is not sufficient for an exterior door. A good-quality spring lock combined with a dead bolt is the bare minimum these days. This makes a forced entry more time-consuming, an effective deterrent since most intruders won't spend more than a minute trying to get into a home.

Dead bolts are a quick and inexpensive way to make your home more secure, and they can be installed quite easily. There are several different types of dead bolts:

SINGLE-CYLINDER DEAD BOLT Operates with a key and is a supplement to a regular house lock. It's called a single cylinder because it operates using a key on the outside and a thumb-turn knob on the inside.

SURFACE-MOUNTED DEAD BOLT   Is the most impervious to jimmying and the easiest to mount on any door. It provides security only when someone is home, however, because the lock is operational only from the inside. A thumb turn slides a vertical bolt into an eye on the striker plate. This lock could be a good choice for your back, garage, or basement doors.

Dead bolts are usually installed 6 in. to 10 in. above the doorknob. Single-cylinder dead bolts are designed to be installed flush with the door. So to install these locks, you have to drill two holes in the door: one for the cylinder and one for the bolt. Most dead bolt sets come with templates to guide the drilling and mortising required.

You will need a "hole" saw to create the large opening needed to install a dead bolt. As you cut the hole, remember to back the drill off periodically, as sawdust may clog the bit. The drill bit needs to enter the door at a 90-degree angle. Ensure this by clamping a wood square to the door so the top of the drill touches it and guides the bit into the door at the right angle. Or, you could use a drill with a built-in level for this job.

Simple Solution

Use tension rods and a fabric panel to cover a window on or adjacent to your front door for added privacy.

Installing a Dead Bolt (in a wood entry door)

WHAT YOU NEED   **Dead bolt** (Some kits will not require all of the following tools. See manufacturer's instructions.)
Tape
Awl
Drill
Safety glasses

Hole saw
Pencil
Wood chisel
Spade bit
Screwdriver
Lipstick

STEP 1   Tape the template from the dead bolt kit to the door at the desired height and use an awl to mark the main hole on the face of the door (to hold the lock in place) and the hole for the bolt in the edge of the door.

STEP 2   Remove the template and drill the main hole in the face of the door using a 2 ⅛ in. hole saw and drill. (Size may vary by manufacturer.) Place the point of the drill bit on the mark and drill only until the point of the bit emerges on the other side of the door. With the drill on slow speed, back the bit out. Move to the other side of the door and use the bit hole as a guide to finish drilling the hole back through the door.

STEP 3   With a 1 in. spade bit (some people refer to these as paddle bits), drill a hole through the edge of door into the main hole (at the point marked from the template).

> ### Simple Solution
>
> **In a pinch, you can use part of a broom handle in your patio door tracks to reinforce your security system.**

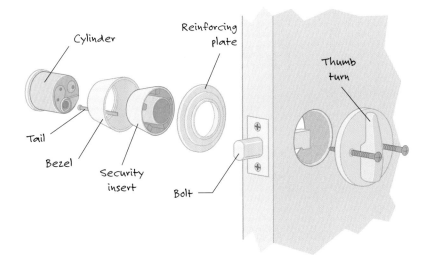

STEP 4   Insert the latch (bolt) and outline the faceplate, then remove and mortise out the area within the outline. Remove enough with the wood chisel so that the faceplate is flush with the edge of the door.

STEP 5   Insert the latch and faceplate and secure them to the edge of the door using the screws included with the dead bolt set.

STEP 6   Install the portion of the cylinder assembly that will go on the outside of the door. In most cases, this is accomplished by holding it upright in one hand and turning the tailpiece (the long, narrow piece that connects the inside and outside cylinder) to align with the crescent-shaped opening in the latch mechanism. Twist into place.

STEP 7   Insert the interior assembly by grasping it in one hand with the *top* facing up. Align and insert tailpiece and swivel to push the assemblies together. (Have some patience here; some just do not line up easily.)

STEP 8   Install screws that connect and secure the cylinders together. (Apply a tiny drop of liquid thread locker to each screw before installing to keep them from loosening.)

STEP 9   Find the exact spot on the door frame to drill the hole for the bolt by rubbing the end of the bolt with lipstick, closing the door, and turning the bolt several times. The lipstick will leave a mark where the bolt hits the door frame.

STEP 10 Place the point of the 1 in. spade bit right in the middle of the lipstick mark and drill a 1 in. deep hole. Close the door and check to see that the bolt fits the hole. Then drill the hole deeper or larger as necessary.

STEP 11 Place the striker plate over the hole and trace around the edge using a pencil. Now use the chisel again to mortise this area for the striker plate until it is flush with the edge of the door frame.

STEP 12 Drill pilot holes and secure the striker plate with 3 in. screws.

Installing a Rim Lock Dead Bolt

WHAT YOU NEED **Dead bolt**   **Awl**
Drill   **Wood chisel**
Pencil   **Screwdriver**
Safety glasses

STEP 1   Drill a hole for the cylinder, following the directions above, and insert the cylinder from the outside. Position the mounting plate on the inside of the door and secure to the cylinder.

STEP 2   Mark screw holes for the lock case, drill pilot holes, and secure the lock case to the mounting plate and door.

STEP 3   Close the door until the protruding portion of the lock case touches the trim of the door frame. Mark where the top and bottom of the lock case touch the door frame.

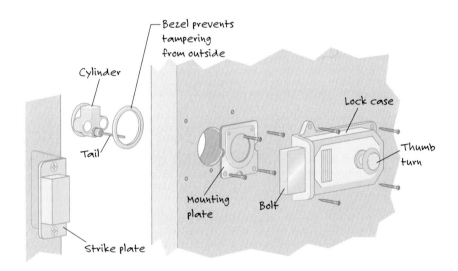

STEP 4   Position the striker plate between the marks for the lock case, and mark the vertical edge of the striker plate. Use a wood chisel to remove trim within the lines until the plate fits flush and is in line with the inside door edge.

STEP 5   Position the striker again, drawing the outline on the doorjamb. Chisel out the thickness of the striker plate and secure with screws.

For a surface mount dead bolt lock, omit step 1.

Rekeying Locks

When you move into a new home, it's always a good idea to change the locks; who knows how many people have keys to "your" home? It might not be necessary, though, to get a new lock: If it's a good-quality dead bolt, you probably can just rekey it and save some money. Most single-cylinder locks can be rekeyed with kits available at hardware stores. You'll need to know the brand name of your lock in order to purchase the appropriate rekeying kit. In most cases the brand name will be stamped on the lock cylinder.

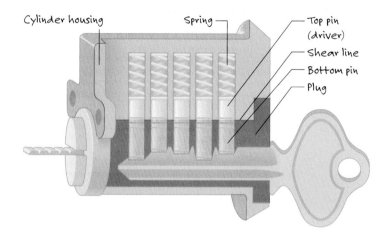

Though the actual directions will vary, depending on the manufacturer, the general idea is always the same. Inside the lock a number of cylinder holding pins create a profile that fits a certain key. By replacing the tiny pins with those of different lengths and sizes, you change the profile and therefore the key needed to open it. This project takes a steady hand and lots of patience.

STEP 1 Remove the lock set from the door.

STEP 2 Next, remove the cylinder and holding pins. The best way to go about this is with the follower tool included in the rekeying kit.

STEP 3 The new key set will have color-coded pins. Install them as directed by the color code for the individual kit you have (each kit, of course, has a different key from the next, thus a unique code).

STEP 4 Reassemble the lock.

Windows

Now, let's take a look at how well your windows are equipped for protecting you from unwanted guests and the elements.

You might think that you have locking windows, when what you really have is window latches. It's important to realize that the latches on your windows are designed not to keep out intruders, but to keep the windows tightly closed against the wind. In fact, a burglar willing to break the glass can simply reach through, unlatch the window, and get into your house within seconds.

The good news is that window latches can be replaced with key-operated latches or supplemented with locking pins, security bolts, track stops, or track stops with keys. All of these options are relatively inexpensive and will greatly increase the security of your home.

Key-operated window latches can be installed on double-hung, casement, and sliding windows and patio doors. Some key latches are sold with one-way screws that make it impossible for an intruder to remove them. This is such a good idea that I'd recommend buying one-way screws if your lock set doesn't include them.

An important word of warning about key-operated window locks: Locks on windows not only make it difficult to get in, they make it difficult to get out. Further, they may go against your local housing code; you'll want to investigate that before installing them. In any case, keep in mind that they could impede your family's need to exit the house quickly in an emergency.

If you decide to install any type of security system on your windows, make sure that each family member knows how to operate it. In the case of key locks, keep the key near each window in a place where each family member can quickly retrieve it. For example, you might hang the key on a small cup hook that's installed underneath the windowsill and the drapery, carefully hidden from outside view.

Replacing Window Locks

When replacing existing window locks with key-operated locks, make sure the window is closed tight. Remove the old latch, position the new one, and mark screw holes with an awl. Of course, you can feel free to use the screw holes from the old latch if they align with the screw holes on the new locks. If the holes are too big, fill them with wooden toothpicks, matchsticks, or wood shavings coated with wood glue (pack the screw hole as tightly as you can). Let the patch dry and then you can sand and drill new pilot holes.

Installing Homemade Window Peg Latches

WHAT YOU NEED **Drill and bits**
Finishing nails (long enough to go through the lower sash and three quarters of the way through the upper sash plus ³⁄₁₆ in.)
Safety glasses

STEP 1 Close and latch the window and drill a hole slightly larger than the finishing nail in the upper corners of the lower window sash, drilling about three quarters of the way into the lower corners of the upper window sash.

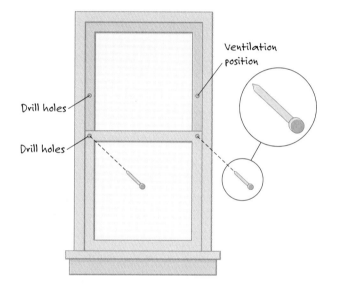

STEP 2 Raise the window about 3 in. or 4 in. and repeat the drilling step, going through the holes you just drilled in the upper corner of the lower sash and into the side sash of the upper window.

STEP 3 Insert the nails. Now you can secure the window in both the closed and open position.

Security Rods

Spring-action tension security bars can help to secure doors or windows of all sizes. Some of the more elaborate ones have a motion sensor that sounds an alarm or lights up, or both, when triggered. These bars are also able to withstand over 1,000 lbs. of pressure.

One night when all of us happened to be out, two of my kids arrived home and heard a noise coming from Angel's second-floor bedroom. When they got up there, they discovered that someone had been trying to break in through the window by standing on the roof of the first floor. (This was the same night the neighbor down the street was robbed.) The would-be burglar fled at the sound of Angel and Vince returning to the house. We promptly installed motion-sensitive tension bars in all of the upstairs windows. You, too, might consider them for double-hung windows, horizontal sliders, and patio doors.

Who's Out There?

Indoors and out, light is one of your best defenses against intruders. But if fear of an exorbitant electric bill is keeping your home in the dark, consider motion-sensitive lights. You can even find a special socket that will screw into your existing lamp base and convert it into a motion-sensitive one. They don't require any special wiring because it's already housed in the special socket.

Outside your home, consider installing surface-mounted, solar-powered, motion-detecting lights. They're energy-efficient and ecologically friendly additions to your home security system. You can install them in areas where there are no electrical hookups—sunlight is all they require.

I have light fixtures at each of the back entrances that have photocells that automatically turn the lights on at dusk and off at dawn. We also have low-voltage lighting integrated into our landscaping and deck designs and plugged into timers. These fixtures light the way for us, but they also deter intruders who don't care to be caught "in the spotlight."

Sound the Alarm

Before you invest in a home security system, consider carefully what's available. These systems range from very simple alarms that alert neighbors and scare away intruders to quite complicated and pricey devices that dial up security offices or your local police department. The more elaborate systems usually require a professional to hardwire the alarm into your home's electrical system (although it is not impossible to do yourself). A control center monitors the alarm's signals for an additional monthly fee.

If you don't want to pay for a professionally installed alarm system, do-it-yourselfers can purchase a wireless system that offers the basics and allows for continuous upgrades and expansion. These systems generally have a console that plugs into an outlet in a central location in your home and transmits and receives signals via a radio frequency. The alarm that sounds is somewhat louder than a smoke detector. Strategically placed transmitters at potential entry points trigger a siren when a break-in is detected, and there are also sensors that mount on glass that will sound if the window is broken.

These sensors are a particularly good idea for sliding patio doors or large windows that could be easily entered by smashing the glass.

Some other features to pay attention to when shopping for your alarm system include the volume of the alarm, a remote control feature, a back-up battery in case of power failure, external sirens, lamp flasher alarms, and motion sensors. The more elaborate do-it-yourself systems will even dial the police. There's a lot to think about when investing in an alarm system.

Once you've selected your system, the first step for most is to begin by setting a code for the system so that all components are functioning on the same radio frequency. Follow the manufacturer's instructions. Note: The transmitters for most wireless systems can be permanently mounted using screws; however, if you are a renter and want to take the devices with you when you leave, install them with double-sided tape included with most systems.

Simple Solution

Make sure your kids check through the peephole and know a visitor before opening a door. Let them know it's better to risk hurting a stranger's feelings than to risk their own safety.

Installing a Wireless Alarm System

WHAT YOU NEED   **Wireless alarm set**   **Screwdriver**
                            Double-sided tape   **Drill and bits** (if installing permanently)
                            Safety glasses

Directions will vary from system to system. In general, though, these are the basic steps that you'll take:

STEP 1   Mount the door and window transmitters using double-sided tape (or screws—drill pilot holes first).

STEP 2   The magnetic part of the transmitter should be attached to the frame of the door or window and the sensor portion installed directly on the door or window sash. You'll see arrows on both the transmitter and sensors: make sure these arrows are aligned and facing each other and that they are no more than $\frac{1}{4}$ in. apart when the door or window is in the closed position.

STEP 3   Activate the alarm system.

Who Is it?

It's always a good idea to know who's on the other side of the door before you open it. Luckily, if your door doesn't have a peephole, it's really easy to install one yourself. Make sure to position it on the door so that all members of the family can easily use it. A household with young children might want two peepholes at different heights.

The peephole comes in two parts. One part is installed from the outside of the door and threaded into the second part which is installed from the inside.

Installing a Peephole

WHAT YOU NEED   **Peephole**   **Measuring tape**
                            Drill   **Pencil/awl**
                            Spade (paddle) bit   **Liquid thread locker**
                            Masking tape   **Safety glasses**

STEP 1   On the inside of the door, use a pencil to mark the location where the peephole will be installed.

STEP 2   Using a spade bit, in the size recommended by the manufacturer, begin drilling a hole on the inside of the door. When the point of the spade bit pierces through the other side, stop drilling and move to the outside.

Drill at the point made by the drill bit tip until the bit goes completely through the door.

STEP 3 Lightly sand the rough edges of the hole on both sides.

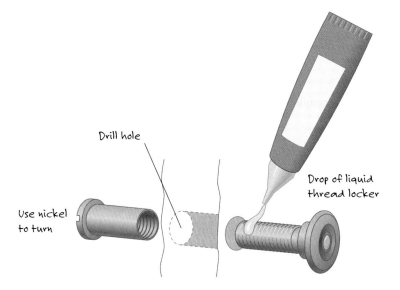

Drill hole

Use nickel to turn

Drop of liquid thread locker

STEP 4 Place a tiny drop of liquid thread locker on the threads of the peephole and insert the two pieces of the peephole through the hole in the door. Remember that the side with the groove gets positioned on the inside of the door.

STEP 5 Use a nickel as a screwdriver and tighten the two parts together.

Protection against Household Hazards

We've seen how you can protect yourself and your family against intruders and the elements, but dangers can lurk inside too. A safe and secure home is one that's properly maintained and prepared for any emergency.

Carbon Monoxide

Carbon monoxide is a killer you can neither see nor smell, a by-product of fuel-burning devices. It is impossible to completely avoid exposure to this gas: you want to guard against dangerous levels.

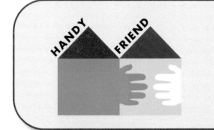

Chief Charles Burns of the Chicago Fire Department provides this helpful tip: "One thing that you want to do with smoke detectors is to regularly vacuum the areas where dust and debris can collect. In doing that, you'll keep the sensors clean and they'll be able to better serve you."

A malfunctioning furnace or a car left running in the garage are the two most common sources of harmful amounts of carbon monoxide in the home. But gas water heaters, kitchen stoves, fireplaces, fuel-burning room heaters, wood stoves, charcoal grills, and even your power lawn mower can emit carbon monoxide.

Watch for these warning signs of harmful carbon monoxide buildup:

- Soot accumulating around the outside of the chimney, furnace, fireplace, or woodstove.
- Disconnected or decaying vent or chimney pipes on water heaters, furnaces, and woodstoves.
- Blocked chimney openings or clogged chimneys.
- Very high humidity in the house, often showing up as moisture on the windows.
- No draft in the chimney or a hot draft from the chimney into the home.
- The smell of exhaust fumes in the home or stuffy, stale, or smelly air that never clears.

To prevent dangerous levels of carbon monoxide:

- Never insulate or block the venting mechanism on any fuel-burning appliance. Check them regularly to be sure there are no blockages.
- Don't obstruct the circulation of air around appliances.
- Keep furnace panels and grills in place. Be sure the fan compartment door is closed when the furnace is operating.
- Have your fuel-burning equipment checked periodically by a qualified service technician.
- Do not run vehicles in a closed garage.
- Do not use a barbecue grill indoors.
- Don't use a cooking stove or oven to heat the home.
- No home insulation job is complete without checking to see if extra ventilation is necessary.
- Furnaces should be inspected by a professional every year.

Don't Risk It

Two types of detectors monitor the presence of carbon monoxide: chemical and electrical. Chemical detectors change color in the presence of carbon monoxide; you have to check them regularly because they do not sound an alarm. Electrical detectors sound an alarm in response to a dangerous level of carbon monoxide.

Battery-operated electrical detectors mount to the ceiling like smoke detectors. Plug-in detectors are powered when plugged into any 110/120-volt wall outlet. Most have a battery backup in the event of a power failure. If you are going to install only one detector, it should be located near the bedrooms. Ideally, each floor of a home should have a carbon monoxide detector.

Ready for Anything

In spite of your best efforts, you may find yourself facing a household fire. Keep a fire extinguisher on hand: If you are only going to have one fire extinguisher, buy one that is rated for all types of fires. You'll want to make sure everyone in the family knows how to use it. Teach them the **PASS** word for using fire extinguishers:

P—pull the pin (if there is one)
A—aim the nozzle
S—squeeze the lever
S—sweep the base of the fire

Use a fire extinguisher only on small, contained fires and make sure you have access to an exit in the event the fire goes out of control. Never, ever, rely on a fire extinguisher to save a life; if the extinguisher isn't doing anything to the fire, get out!

Installing a Fire Extinguisher

WHAT YOU NEED **Fire extinguisher**   **Drill**
               Pencil/awl   **Screwdriver**
               Safety glasses

Position the fire extinguisher's hanging bracket and mark screw holes with a pencil or awl. Drill holes to accommodate the anchors normally included with the unit. Insert the anchors, reposition the bracket, and install the screws. Hang the extinguisher in the bracket. Follow the manufacturer's suggestions for regular testing of this equipment.

Every family should have a plan of escape in the event of fire, including a meeting point outside and away from the house. Every family member should know the phone number of the fire department (most parts of the country have activated the 911 emergency number, but not all). Autodial telephones should be programmed with these and other emergency numbers. Once or twice a year, you should hold a surprise fire drill so that your family knows how to respond in the face of an emergency.

Smoke Detectors

Every home should have at least one smoke detector on each level, including the basement and attic. Place them at the top of each flight of stairs. Ranch-style homes and apartments should have one in the living area and one in the bedroom area.

Test the smoke detectors at least once a month. Press the button to see if the horn is working; then, from beneath the detector, light a match and blow it out to make sure the device actually detects and reacts to smoke.

Every once in a while, test the alarm in the middle of the night to see if all family members respond. I tested my family's fire safety readiness one night, setting off the alarm and waiting to see what happened. What a lesson in reality that was. My kids didn't get up; they didn't even stir in their beds! They slept right through that loud noise. If this is a problem in your home, it's a good idea to install a smoke detector on the ceiling inside the door in each child's room.

Installing a Battery-Operated Smoke Detector

WHAT YOU NEED

Battery-operated smoke detector	Anchors
Pencil/awl	Screwdriver
Drill and bit	Battery
Safety glasses	

Remove or open the housing and position the smoke detector mounting plate. Mark the screw holes with a pencil. Drill a hole to accommodate the anchors included with the unit. Insert the anchors, position the detector over the anchors, and install the screws. Connect the battery and close the housing.

PLAY IT
SAFE!

• Enroll in a self-defense course at your local community college or center.

• Coach your children in self-defense techniques.

• Make sure your children know not to tell strangers, either on the phone or at the front door, that their parents aren't home.

• Only use cash machines that are in well-lit, busy neighborhoods, and avoid using them late at night.

• Encourage your children to travel in pairs.

• Always make sure that you and your family have personal identification with you as you travel about.

• If you or your family members have an important medical condition, consider getting a medical-alert bracelet tag.

• Don't play the hero: call in emergency experts.

Handy Resources

The World Wide Web is one of the best new tools for do-it-yourselfers! Now, you can find yourself just a mouse click away from discovering valuable information and resources. In this section, we'll introduce you to some of our favorite sites on the Web. As soon as you begin surfing, you're bound to uncover even more exciting places to check out. Believe me, every time I plan to quickly log on and just look for one piece of information, two hours later I'm still working my way through one fascinating site or another. There's so much to explore!

Now before the advent of the Web, of course, I got some of my handiest information from fellow do-it-yourselfers and publications. You should start by adding to your library how-to books about your particular interest or project at hand. Here's just a couple that can be helpful as resources: One is *The Complete Illustrated Guide to Everything Sold in Hardware Stores* by Steve Ettinger—an illustrated guide to all those odd, wonderful, and necessary things in the hardware stores and home centers. There's also a series of decorating books called *Arts & Crafts for Home Decorating*® by the Home Decorating Institute. Just take a walk through a bookstore or library—you'll be amazed at all the help there is for you. In addition, there are many magazines that have the latest in home improvement updates, such as *The Family Handyman. Good Houskeeping Do It Yourself* is an all-around magazine that appeals to anyone interested in decorating, craft, and home improvement, and in my column in that magazine I not only answer readers' questions, I also share my do-it-yourself real-life experiences. I'm a firm believer that we can really learn from fellow do-it-yourselfers, so if you don't have any HandyFriends yet, it's time to make some. Actually, all you need to do is bring up the fact that you are thinking of doing this or that at your next social gathering, and people will be coming out of the woodwork to offer advice. You may find yourself starting your own HandyGroup! It'd be a great place to share and collect advice (not to mention war stories).

Handy Web Sites

General Information

WWW.TODAYSHOMEOWNER.COM features a wide variety of home projects, from electrical to gardening ideas. Click on their electrical and lighting icon, for example, and you'll find a wealth of information, from how to suppress a voltage surge to making your halogen lamps safer.

WWW.DOITYOURSELF.COM is a huge site with information about home projects, big and small. Say you're interested in changing your kitchen floor? Well, then you'd click on **Floor Coverings** and there you'd find a library of flooring books, a listing of other Web sites, and a **Do-it-Yourself Floor Covering Q&A**. It's quite a handy resource!

WWW.HOUSENET.COM is the ultimate site for do-it-yourselfers. They have a library of articles on subjects ranging from home repair to arts and crafts, plus informative columns from various experts. If you have a question on just about any subject you can post it in one of the chat rooms or send a question to one of the advisers online. In the **Message Board** area you can see visitors' questions and answers or add your own advice. You can also submit a question to be answered by a HouseNet Advisor and other visitors. Just go to the **Message Board** section of the Web site, and, for example, if you click on the **Home Improvement** link, you can share remodeling and home repair advice. One of the first home improvement Web sites, this site was started by my friends Katie and Gene Hamilton as a hobby several years ago, and it has taken off.

Handy Tools

WWW.HOMECENTRAL.COM is a great home improvement site, but what we like most of all is its extremely handy, illustrated tool dictionary. Did you just read about a project calling for some tool you've never heard of? Well, click on this site's appropriate tool category (hand tools, power tools, specialty tools, or rental tools) and you can find your way to an illustration of your mystery tool.

Electrical

WWW.NESF.ORG is the site of the national electrical safety foundation, a not-for-profit organization dedicated to improving electrical safety awareness. Especially if you're just getting started with home improvement, I'd encourage you to take the time to look at the information posted here. They've got some great facts and tips for the home, school, or office—including how to make electrical safety fun and interesting for kids. In addition to safety tips, you also can find educational information, such as how a three-prong plug works.

Walls

WWW.PDRA.ORG is a site provided by the Paint and Decorating Retailers Association. They have very clear guidelines for figuring out how much paint or drywall you'll need for a particular project. And they've got lots of other great consumer advice, such as the answers to frequently asked questions about wallcoverings and paint. I really like the easy-to-understand illustrations in the Q&A section.

WWW.LISP.WAYNE.EDU is the Web site of the Wayne State University Library and Information Science Program. Once there, you can click on **Web Pathfinders** and then on resources for wallpapering and faux painting projects. You'll find tips for planning your wall decorating projects, as well as lots of links to various organizations and companies to help you get the job done.

Furniture Restoration

WWW.FURNITUREWIZARD.COM, as you might guess, is a Web site devoted to furniture repair and refinishing. Click on **Refinishing Techniques** for some great tips on restoring classic furniture. Or try clicking on the **Furniture Repair Strategies** for some savvy fix-up ideas. One more spot to see: the **Hot Question Showcase** where the Furniture Wizard answers queries from his guests.

Bathroom/Kitchen Plumbing

WWW.THEPLUMBER.COM features a wealth of information about plumbing for both do-it-yourselfers and professionals. The page has a strong **Frequently Asked Question (FAQ)** section with information ranging from common plumbing abbreviations to tips on fixing low-flush toilets and slow-running drains. The site has links to *Plumbing and Mechanical Magazine*, where you can access even more data.

WWW.KITCHEN-BATH.COM has a really ingenuous **Doctor in the House** page where kitchen and bath experts answer some common questions. It also has lots of bath and kitchen design ideas. And it provides information about a wide variety of products from many different manufacturers, giving you an idea of what's available in a variety of price ranges.

WWW.TOILETOLOGY.COM displays perhaps the best collection of household puns on the Web with its: "Plunge right in, flush out the facts and plumb the depths of toilet repairs." (You can stop groaning now.) And you'll admire their enthusiastic pledge to tell you "almost everything you ever wanted to know about your toilets!" Seriously, in their **Toiletology 101** section, they do have comprehensive information about everything from how a toilet works to what causes "lazy flushing."

Home Organization

WWW.TGON.COM belongs to "The Get Organized News." The site has information-packed articles on issues ranging from the very broad question of "How do I get started?" to more specific sticklers like "How do I clean out my closet?" It provides fast links to other clutter-busting sites.

Decorating and Crafts for the Home

WWW.INETEX.COM/NOME/ contains fun activities for the whole family. This site has a whole bunch of games that you and your kids can make and play together. Or if you are planning a party, this site has lots of tips to help. In addition, you can find many general decorating tips and craft projects for your home.

WWW.WIN.NET/~WNC/CPROJECT.HTML is the Wood n' Crafts online site where you can find additional craft projects. Once at the home page, click on **Craft Projects** to see a list of what's available. This site also has links to many other craft sites. There is even a link to get free craft patterns.

Home Energy

WWW.EPA.GOV/ENERGYSTAR is the location of the U.S. Environmental Protection Agency's energy star program, which is the EPA's initiative to support company's manufacture, promotion, and use of energy-efficient equipment. You've probably seen the energy star on computers, TVs, VCRs, and other appliances. If you go to this site, you can find out how those products will help you save energy.

WWW.HOMEENERGY.ORG is *Home Energy Magazine*'s Web site. This magazine is published by a non-profit organization whose goal is to provide information on residential energy conservation. You can look at back issues of the magazine with its articles on everything from lamps to heating and cooling to home remodeling tips. There are also links to other energy-related sites.

Your Yard

WWW2.GARDEN.ORG/NGA is the official site for the National Gardening Association. It's got lots of features to help you plant and maintain your garden. For example, it relays detailed information about plants and their various uses, such as aromatherapy, healing and medicinal herbs, and edible plants. Plus, you can link up to regional gardening and botanical associations.

WWW.HOMECENTRAL.COM/HOWTO surf on back to the **Home Central** site for information *before* you start that major yard project. There, for instance, you can find directions on building your own deck! By clicking on the deck icon you'll get the steps you need to guide you through the entire process from start to finish.

Home Safety

WWW.GETSAFE.COM is a site with hard facts and tips about both crime and fire safety. For example, did you know that 38 precent of all assaults occur during home invasions? It also suggests a number of no-cost, low-cost ways to help harden your security. And from here, you can link up to **McGruff the Crime Dog** and to the **FBI's Crime Statistics Report.**

WWW.NFPA.ORG is the Web site of the National Fire Protection Association. It maintains up-to-date information about fire safety, including the latest on smoke detectors and carbon monoxide detectors. Also, read stories from their famed **Learn Not to Burn** educational program, which is credited with saving countless lives.

Consumer Protection

WWW.HUD.GOV gives you links to other government sites that contain consumer protection and consumer product safety information.

WWW.DOC.GOV/BUREAUS offers a link called **Consumer Affairs**, which provides tips on how to resolve complaints and tells you where you can order consumer guides on various subjects.

Index